# FURTHER AGONY

## ONE MORE ROUND WITH SYKES

Jamie Boyle

I would like to dedicate this book to my beautiful Son, Jameson Lennon Boyle. You make my life worth living, you're my pride and joy and I love you more than Morrissey hates everything. God bless you Son. All my love always, Love Daddy xxx

**WARCRY PRESS**

ISBN: 978 0995531260

Original cover illustration & design by James Ryan Foreman
www.jamesryanforeman.com

Poetry by: Chris Campbell and Jack W Gregory

Find out more at: facebook.com/furtheragony

Printed and bound in Great Britain by Clays Ltd, St Ives plc

## ACKNOWLEDGEMENTS

I would like to take the time to thank everyone who contributed to the research for this book and the chapters therein, giving special thanks to the following:

The Wakefield Express, The Yorkshire Post, CEO's of Warcry Press Boris and Floyd and their minions, James Ryan Foreman, Matt Hamilton, Simon Ambler, Jack W Gregory, Chris Campbell, Gavin Hepworth, David Flint, the residents of Wakefield and last but not least my lovely Wife Shirley-anne Boyle.

## THE BRADLEY LOWERY FOUNDATION

Registered Charity Number: 1174333

£1 from the sale of each publication will be donated to the Bradley Lowery Foundation.

**John Conteh MBE**

*WBC World Champion 1974-1978*

I met Paul Sykes a few times on the boxing scene, a few times in London with Alex Steene and once or twice in gyms.

It is truly remarkable that after 13 years in Prison on a diet of porridge, bread and water that Paul came out of Prison to fight for the British and Commonwealth titles at an age when most fighters are retired. I myself had been retired and finished for 4 years by the time Paul fought John L Gardner.

To come from the background that he was involved in and box for them titles is an achievement in itself.

Boxing was Paul's real talent and it's just a shame he never used it and that he's more well known for other things than boxing.

Paul had 2 years at boxing and he gave it a go as much as he could.

**Richy Horsley (Crazy Horse)**

*Author of 'Born to Fight.*
*The True Story of Richy (Crazy Horse) Horsley'*

Paul Sykes' toughness and courage were second to none.
You only have to watch his fight with John L Gardner for
the British and Commonwealth titles to see how tough he
was. Those six rounds were non-stop action and they were
both landing bombs. You don't get a shot at a British title
if you haven't got any boxing ability. Sykes was one tough
hombre.

**Richard Dunn**

*English former Heavyweight, World Title challenger and European Champion*

I remember Sykesy and he had one hell of an interesting life.

I heard about Paul Sykes whilst I was still an amateur in the 1960's. The things I would hear about him were of this big rough lad always getting into bother.

I went along to spar with Paul Sykes once in Doncaster. When I sparred with him, from my point of view, it was only one round and I stayed in second gear, Sykesy on the other hand was trying to take my head off with every punch he threw. Every time Paul sparred with anyone he tried to bully them and roll over the top of them. Sometimes he got away with it and sometimes people stood up to him like I did and he didn't like that at all. Paul always wanted it all his own way in the ring and of course the fight game is not like that.

If Paul Sykes would have behaved himself he'd have done alright in the ring to be quite truthful. Sykesy was a big strong lad and he could dig but he always tried to take it that bit too far in sparring. If he had been 'normal' he'd have done very well as he had the ability but of course he wasn't normal.

No two people are the same and he certainly wasn't.

**Bunny Johnson**

*British and Commonwealth Heavyweight Champion*

I sparred with Paul Sykes in 1973 at the Thomas A Beckett
Gym. Paul was contracted to spar with Joe Frazier.
Anyway, Frazier was having a break from sparring and at
the time I was the main contender for a shot at the British
Title and Paul told me to get in the ring and spar a few
rounds with him to check out my capabilities. He was a
tough man and he relished being tough and being thought
of as tough. We had a good sparring session. I remember
it very well because he compared my punching power to
that of the dynamic Joe Frazier.

I found Paul to be a very hard man as a boxer in the ring.
He was someone I felt I could trust. He was an intelligent
man who did not support the lack of opportunities for
black fighters at the time.

*"I'm the only man in the history of mankind that has swum across the straights of Johor.*

*Not because of the currents, nothing like that.*

*It's sharks.*

*It's not shark infested, but none of the locals go paddling.*

*I know about sharks, I know about sharks yeah.*
*I know how to do 'em, you punch em right in the fucking ear'ole and they swim off."*

**-P Sykes**

# CONTENTS

# INTRODUCTION

Jamie Boyle

Sykes-Unfinished Agony came out on Tuesday March 7th 2017, ten years exactly to the day that Paul Sykes passed away.

The lost son of Lupset was a complete one off and Wakefield will never see his like again. When Paul Sykes died it was the end of an era for Wakefield, a place I've grown fond of and now will in some way always feel attached to.

I have had a mixed reaction to Unfinished Agony coming out, most people congratulated me and said it was a really insightful unbiased view about Paul though at the other end of the scale I've had a death threat or two! You can't please everyone though can you and if you want to make an omelette you must break a few eggs!

Not everyone was overjoyed about me waking up the sleeping ghost of Paul Sykes and I've had my fair share of 'trolls' on social media but when you discover Paul Sykes, there's so many questions and queries that you're left with but there's so little to go on. Speaking from personal experience I can understand why people become so curious about who he was and what he was about and I've spoken to many people over the last five years who have also become as intrigued with him as I had become.

I wasn't born until 1980 which means I wasn't born when he carried out most of his evil acts of violence some of which impacted on people's lives greatly, it's almost as if some people hold me accountable for that.

Even though we are now two books into speaking about Paul with people who knew him, I'm still learning about him and discovering that people's hatred or people's love for Paul haven't diminished over the last ten years.

I never really had any plans to do a second book and it wouldn't have come about at all if I hadn't heard from the very eloquent and charismatic Mr. Delroy Showers, who I liked a great deal and who was such a good friend of Paul's and I'd like to thank Delroy personally for his insight into Paul and who he was.

Another insightful view about Paul came from Janet Sellers and her son Mark and I appreciate how hard it was for her to speak about Paul and hope that now in a cathartic sense Janet can now put those demons about a man who made her life and that of her family's life hell to rest. Initially Janet refused to even consider giving us an interview but then thought, "No, I'm not allowing him to still dictate to me about my life after being dead for ten years". After Janet gave the interview in the offices of Warcry Press I noticed that Janet become quite emotional and even commented that she felt like a weight had finally been lifted after all these years.

Another person I feel I must mention also is Julie Allott. I encountered Julie on one of the Paul Sykes Facebook pages as she messaged me to tell me that she had found a flyer for the first book in the front garden of her business office. Julie ordered the book and really enjoyed reading about a man she knew only too well from the Wakefield Magistrates Court. Thank you for your time Julie I know that you are a ridiculously busy lady.

I would also like to mention David Flint who is the Grandson of the flamboyant Dennis Flint. I discovered through talking to various people over the last few years that they have been just as interested in Dennis as they have been with Paul and nobody had really heard anything of him since the documentary, certainly if you Google Dennis, very little comes up.

When I met up with the producers of Paul Sykes at Large in December 2015 in The Majestic Hotel in Harrogate with Paul's only sibling Kay, the producers both told me how funny and interesting they thought Dennis Flint was. They went on to tell me that the scene of

Paul knocking on Dennis' door asking, "Are you in Dennis me auld Pal?" then hearing Dennis laugh and seeing him sat there with the cigar and wig sat behind that Rolls Royce desk was purposely filmed in that order for maximum comedy value and I think they got that bang on.

I had never given Wakefield much thought before I watched Paul Sykes at Large back in 2012, it was one of those places like Milton Keynes or Coventry, you knew they existed but didn't know anything about them places. So, the people that have said that in some way Paul Sykes put Wakefield on the map I must somewhat agree with. I have a real liking for Wakefield though now I have visited it several times, it is a place steeped in proud Yorkshire history and the Cathedral is something else entirely. Myself and my Wife spent quite some time there when we visited in March 2016, it's beautiful and if anyone is visiting Wakefield I urge them to go and have a look.

There's someone who stood out in the first book for his help and he didn't disappoint me in the help that he gave me with this second one and he is Chris Campbell. I haven't spoken to anyone from Wakefield that doesn't know him and everyone that I have spoken to had only good things to say about him, I want to thank you for the time and effort you have put into these books Chris, you Sir are a full-time legend and who would have thought you'd be fantastic at poetry too!

So, you're about to read over thirty more chapters about Paul Sykes. His name is getting more and more familiar in the last few years since my interest in him began. Would I have liked Paul Sykes if I'd have grown up in the City of Wakefield? Probably not, must be my honest answer. Would I have found him a figure of interest if I'd lived in Wakefield? Hell yes!

I imagine that if you've bought this second book, that has come out six months to the day after the first one, that you've read the first book and if you haven't, why not? Go get it! But if you've read the first one then you will know my feelings towards Paul and the reasoning behind these books. I'm not here to do a dead man a wrong deed or to glorify him in any way.

So, go ahead and read more tales from people that knew Paul, hear what they have to say about the 'Wildman of Wakefield' because they knew him, some more than others and he had a very varying impact on the lives on the interviewee's. Once again, make up your own mind about him.

One more thing, I must add is as with the first book a pound from every book sale is going to a registered charity, this time to the Bradley Lowery Foundation. Anyone who hasn't been hid under a rock for the last few months will have heard of the beautiful and inspiring Bradley Lowery, the little six-year-old Sunderland supporter from Blackhall Colliery near Hartlepool who's smile could light up a thousand towns and who's plight touched the lives of so many people and who sadly passed away July 7th 2017 after a courageous battle with Neuroblastoma. Bradley was first diagnosed with Neuroblastoma at the age of 18 months and battled it for over 2 years until he was at last successful and went into remission. In July 2016, sadly Bradley relapsed. Although unfortunately it was too late for Bradley to benefit from the money raised for him, his parents have started the Bradley Lowery Foundation to help other youngsters facing the same terrible diagnosis.

I was asked recently why I would associate Bradley with the likes of Paul Sykes and to that I say I believe that in every negative there is a positive and although Paul Sykes led a very negative existence, I hope by writing about this I can create a positive which is to raise money for such a worthwhile cause as Bradley touched so many lives including my own. Bradley will never be forgotten not only for his courage and his bravery but for that smile. XX

Many thanks, always a pleasure

Jamie Liam Boyle

# DELROY SHOWERS

If you Google the name Paul Sykes then you'll find that Delroy Showers' name will not be too far behind Paul Sykes' in the results.

The Paul Sykes Story is snowballing as you read this very book, why? You may ask yourself, well my theory to the growing interest is that the Paul Sykes at Large documentary is reaching people far and wide, more people are watching it, just as I did in 2012 and those people are as intrigued as I am to find out what happened to Paul next and before my first book 'Unfinished Agony' came out, other than Sweet Agony which Paul wrote himself and the documentary I found that in 2012 there actually wasn't that much more I could find out about him just from searching his name, so I did as Paul himself did, I went out and I had a look!

People will know the name of Delroy Showers from Sweet Agony. I've read that book twice and it's as clear as the day is long that Paul absolutely idolised his best friend Delroy.

Who can forget the chaotic scenes at Paul and Cath's wedding on Paul Sykes at Large! Delroy had been asked to be the Master of Ceremonies but we all saw how that panned out!

From a personal point of view, I tried for many years to get in contact with Delroy and I would have loved to have included him in Unfinished Agony. I didn't realise it at the time but the reason my searches had been so fruitless was that Delroy was finishing his last big sentence of 14 years in Full Sutton near York. Still, better late than never and I was over the moon when I eventually did get given his number. I thought the hardest part was still to come though, I was going to have to bite the bullet and phone Mr. Showers and explain who I was and exactly why

I was phoning him. All I could do was to try to be my most persuasive in the hope that he would see that I didn't have an ulterior motive and I certainly wasn't the old bill!

After speaking with Delroy a couple of times he granted me, what turned out to be, a very thorough and lengthy interview about his old friend Paul Sykes. I was extremely grateful to Delroy for his time and his willingness to speak with me, after all this man was classed in the media as a crime lord along with his older brother Michael. It is fair to say that Delroy Showers was at the top of his game once upon a time as an international drug trafficker.

We agreed to meet at the very plush Grand Queens hotel in Leeds and the first thing that struck me about Delroy was how powerful and fit he looked for a man of 66 years of age, he was very alert, very aware of everything and I could tell he was taking everything in. Having spoken to Delroy I could really relate to Paul's quotes in Sweet Agony saying how articulate Delroy was and how he was the perfect English gentleman.

It was an education to be in his company and he has an aura about him as big as any star that I've met. It's how I imagined a conversation with Chris Eubank would go the words were free flowing.

I hoped I hadn't offended Delroy when I said that he wasn't your everyday ex criminal. He must be one of the most interesting characters that I have ever met in my 37 years on this planet.

\*       \*       \*       \*

It was the latter half of the 60's and I was in my late teens when I heard the name Paul Sykes. I was in prison at the time and the tales of Paul, that I heard in there, were of his numerous fights with prison guards. Paul Sykes was a stand-up veteran fighting man in every sense of the word and he hated the system.

I didn't come across Paul in the flesh until 1970 in Hull prison, Paul walked past me and obviously he'd heard a fair few stories about me too and from that day onwards we were instant brothers from another mother.

Paul Sykes was extremely intelligent and we had struck up an instant friendship. Paul was a very thoughtful person but you could see by looking at him that he'd suffered some problems in his youth, as I had myself. Looking back on the situation now and looking at it from my armchair with hindsight, he was damaged. All the factors of his youth impinged on his character later in his life.

You can't use Paul's parents as the sole excuse for his behaviour but they factor into his irritant behaviour. They can't factor in the lack of control that Paul had that's the weakness of the individual. I've always said my lack of control is down to me, the elements I saw as a child and certain things that happened to me as a child they then became elements explaining my behaviour, you can't explain lack of control.

Paul used to come to a group in Hull Prison which was called The Quaker Group and it was run by a chap called Alan Coursely the founder of Northern Dairies, Northern Foods, the owner of Beverley Beatic Finance Company and The Whole Brewery etc. Alan Coursely was an extremely wealthy Quaker with a very strong social conscience and the Quaker Group in Hull was instrumental in getting all of us into a healthier and more productive way of thinking. When we went to the group we realised the linguistics were not good. This for me, well it made me pay attention as to how I spoke and how I came across to other people. So, I would say it was the Quaker Group in Hull and the folks that were part of it that was instrumental in myself, Eddie Richardson, my brother Michael and Paul becoming much more thoughtful, we got an education in elocution.

I was five years younger than Paul and it's been said that he looked up to me but I'd say that there were area's where he was more refined than me and there were some areas where I had an edge over him because I've always been studious, so on the balance of things Delroy Showers and Paul Sykes was a relationship of absolute equals.

Paul got into fights in Prison, it was a known fact and it wasn't always against prison staff! Paul got into a fight with Chrissy Lambrianou once from the Kray firm that was a running battle on the landing with pans and cutlery. Paul was very cipherous towards the London gangster element. Paul was an extremely proud Yorkshire man.

Paul would teach me the value of Yorkshire history and how it has always been at the root of the military structure in our land. Paul taught me a lot.

I loved Paul's Father and I loved his Mother I was extremely fond of both Walter and Betty Sykes they always made me very welcome at their family home. Paul put them through some difficulties during their lives which was shameful of him.

Paul for me is still a significant feature in my life. The big thing he did for me is that he brought the craziness of my life to an end with the words that he said to me when I saw him in hospital. This was a few months before he died and the scare he had before he went into Pinderfields that final time when he passed away.

I went in to see him and he was laid there very unkempt and in the bad way he was. I said to him "You disappoint me brother living like this, what has happened?". He told me that I hadn't disappointed him and that he still loved me. Then he said something to me that I I'll never forget until my dying day, he said that "It's people like me that allow people like you Delroy, I'm the reason that you have the lifestyle you have with your cars".

I heard that Paul had been living on a boat on a canal and that he was not taking care of his hygiene and I knew from that that he'd slipped because Paul was extremely hygienic. I was living in Argentina at the time and I flew over to see him. He had one or two scares before he died so I thought I'd go and see him to see what I could do, I could even have put him in Argentina or even another part of South America, somewhere where he'd be able to fit into. The whole point of my journey was to save him and put him into rehabilitation with regards to his drinking and his drug taking. So, I went to see him and he could see I was disappointed in him. His condition in general was awful, his physical condition, well you could tell he hadn't trained for many years. I said to Paul words to the effect of "What are you doing this for, why don't you change?" and that's when he looked at me and said the words "If it wasn't for people like me people like you wouldn't be able to drive around in luxury cars". I found this so powerfully arresting, it has been for me a prescript to change.

Those words Paul said to me have been deep in my mind like the grit in the shell of a mollusc the irritant that the grit is, surrounded by material that later transpires to be a pearl! Here was a situation where there it was, a telling, hurtful although truthful statement, I've utilised that as part of my change.

One of the despicable scams Paul and I would pull across different towns was that Paul would dress as a skinhead yob type going into shops owned by Asians and he would act disgustingly racist and kick off often smashing things up and causing mayhem, he was very convincing. I would then turn up about a week later and say that I had heard that they had had some trouble and enquire as to whether I could offer them some protection for their business in return for a small amount of money.

It was deplorable behaviour and my own narcissism twenty years ago, these feelings wouldn't have entered my mind but it was the truth that Paul told me, he told me straight when he was not long for this world and he was right, for me this was very telling and I reminded him of our Quaker friends who I believe planted this sense of order and eventual progressiveness to come out of what had been chaos, just absolute chaos.

I never went to Paul's funeral but I was in the country at the time. I phoned his sister Kay and I told her I was coming but I couldn't go. It was because of many emotional reasons that I couldn't go, his death hit me very hard because Paul and I had been so close, it was hard because Paul was so physically alive and so potent that when they are no longer here it reminds you of your own mortality.

Paul had asked me to officiate at the marriage of himself and his girlfriend Cathy. He knew I'd had several churches over the years, most of them bogus and a way of making finance.

He asked me to come to his home on Gissing Road, Lupset to perform a ceremony. He asked me to don an African attire, my Brother Michael said that I would do no such thing and it would be parody and absurdity rolled into one. So, I came without any native African garb but officiated anyway. The end product was craziness on top of craziness. They weren't classed as married that night because the service didn't continue because Paul was being extremely volatile. I believe they did eventually get married but I wasn't at the wedding, there was talk of him inviting me but I wasn't able to make it for some reason or another. Paul's missus, Cathy, was an angel truly an angel, she was a wonderful human being and I will always love Cath, she thought the world of, my then, Wife Karen.

After the failed wedding attempt we had at Pauls, I got straight off, the reason behind my swift exit was that these big Dutch minders that I had with me wanted to attack Paul. I told them no, that it wasn't going to happen, Paul was family to me! Their argument was "Yeah but he can't do that to you etc.". These guys couldn't have beat Paul in a 50/50 but they wanted to sucker attack him but I told them it wasn't happening and that was that. After the wedding fell apart I felt like a rather large gooseberry.

I wasn't expecting the camera's to be there and when I pulled up and saw all the lights I thought it was a mobile disco, I thought "Oh shit I'm in trouble here". Of course, I had my brother's words in my ear "Don't get involved with anything that will make us look foolish". You can't always be over serious and I think one of the most important things is to be able to laugh at yourself.

Nobody could change my friend Paul. The main thing is that you must be ready for change but the alcohol got in the way with Paul and I think if it wasn't for his drinking he would have been more malleable.

Paul Sykes was intelligent but bruised by his upbringing, like we all are. He was like myself many years ago, too selfish and too narcissistic to see that it's really down to oneself. It's not the system, it's not what you've been through, it's not what you've suffered, these are, of course, factors essentially, it was all down to Paul and I know that because I had the disease myself.

For me now, it's all about trying to reform through looking at myself more clearly. It's selfishness that's what my problem was, Paul had it badly but so did I so I'm not being nasty towards Paul. One of the best defence mechanisms that myself and Paul had was to deny our fallibility and then assume it can't be me, but of course it is you!

Paul was quintessential; he was a serious Yorkshire man. I believe historically that Yorkshire people have been the back bone of all the army's although I do believe Yorkshire did the dirty on Richard III and maybe might have been the cause of his downfall outside in Leicester at the Battle of Boswell. In my opinion Yorkshire people are special people and the backbone of our nation. The professional Yorkshire men are the Kings & Queens of our realm and that's who they've come back to, to maintain power. Other than Scottish people, Yorkshire people have the highest input into all British battles.

I tended to think that Paul was at the wrong age to get to the top echelons when he started boxing at 30. He had the skills but the Jail had forestalled him, that coupled with his emotional state and the drink.

In the John L Gardner fight, there was a lovely bizarre man called Doctor McGill, he's now dead but he was a Blackpool chap and he was giving Paul pure oxygen, of course pure oxygen will make you weaker. Pure oxygen is for use as a recovery element, not to go to war, this would burn resources so it was madness, it was not good.

I remember Don King came to England and had Paul doing some sparring with Larry Holmes, and I tell you now Paul was doing Larry Holmes no favours. They pulled Paul out of the sparring.

I would help Paul sell a lot of tickets during his boxing career and it was me who would sort for him to go to a gym in Toxteth before he went in the ABA's in 1973.

Bi-sexual is a better term, a more descriptive term on Paul's sexuality in prison. It's something he didn't really like to discuss a great deal. Paul would always be the active dominant one in that scenario. Paul would sort 'girlie geezers' to displace his loneliness, he was an active Bi not a passive and I believe that there is a difference.

Paul never pursued that lifestyle outside prison it was only in the nick. It's complex in prison because people don't necessary seek the physicality they seek femininity.

My brother Michael would find this intolerable and it would make him very angry. I used to ask my brother what his problem was regarding this going on in Prison and he would say it was this, this or this, I would say to him "Do you want white folk to have issues about colour? Why do you have issues about sex?".

There were many rumours about myself and Paul Sykes in prison, that we used to ring the bell in Walton, that the guard would come and we'd say, "Officer get us a YP" then they'd bring the YP to our cells then the next morning the YP would get thrown across the landing. This, of course is modern mythology, It's absolutely absurd. None of that is true let me tell you. Many stories over the years about myself and Paul have been utter nonsense.

Most of the gay elements in the Jail is for what feminine males bring to the table. It's the quest for femininity because everybody else would throw shit parcels out of the window, the place is completely full of testosterone. So, imagine that into this testosterone fuelled atmosphere comes a gentle figure who reminds us all of the refinement of life, of the better things of life and of course the femininity because that is the supreme element of what we pursue. So, when a geezer came along with all these elements he was in my posse straight away, but he had to be 7st, blonde and have green eyes!

People ask me if Paul was a successful criminal. Notoriety is success so maybe Paul Sykes was successful.

As for me now, well I don't think it matters if you're in the Bentley. I was in the Bentley but I was a bigger failure than I am now when I'm in a run of the mill car living a clean life. Why was I a bigger failure when I was in the Bentley? Because our children were damaged to put me in that Bentley. So, what is success and what is failure?! We are nothing, then we are something and then we are nothing brothers. I'm 66 now and I don't' know what success and failure is, I think it's just about being alive. I'm in a better place now in my life because I'm straight, I'm in a better place now because I have a cause, in my case that is staying straight and doing something about Islamist Fundamentalists. Also, I like the fact that today, these kids aren't going to bump into smoke that I brought into the country.

So, the Bentley has gone, the wealth has gone, the lifestyle has gone but I'm in a better place because I'm richer. I love being straight, I work hard and I have many projects but all of them are legal and that makes me happy and I can smile because I'm not the bad guy anymore. Now I see it in the eyes of people, when you're black and you're driving around in that Bentley then there's hardworking British folk standing at the bus stop and you're in that car. These people at the bus stop, they know that you're sat there because you're damaging the state, it's an ugly vibe to have. These people at the bus stop are far better than me and I know I cause so much hurt and pain. I remember a policeman once saying to me "I like you Delroy but what you do is very harmful to race relations". I never saw it like that but I understand everything fully now and I'm a better citizen for it.

I fell out with Paul on many occasions over the years. One of the worst things that I ever witnessed him do was put a good lady down. Paul, he went to the News of the World I think it was, I could be wrong but he went to the paper and said something so horrendous about a certain woman. I immediately wrote to Paul and said to him "Paul you are a dirty guy" that was the first really ugly letter that I sent to him. He had described this woman as looking like 'Quasimodo'! This woman was a teacher and she helped a prisoner escape from Hull prison in 1990 and got five years for it. She would bring things in for prisoners, this was a woman who brought potential freedom to people and gave good lives to people, this was a good person! For Paul to then describe her as 'Quasimodo' was terrible, it was terrible! He wrote back of course saying

"Sorry, they misquoted me". I said, "Paul we have to be progressive humans, it's not good you pretending to be friendly with black people then being anti-feminist". I found that very painful and if you ever come across that woman during your research of Paul Sykes' life can you tell her I'm so sorry.

# DAVY DUNFORD

After an introduction from Clyde Broughton we met up with one of Sheffield's original faces Davy Dunford at the Punch Bowl Pub on Hurlfield Rd, Sheffield on the 28th June 2017. Another associate of Paul's and one mentioned in his book Sweet Agony, he'd taken some time to track down, most leads concluded that he was living overseas.

A career criminal, burglar, safe blower, smuggler, Davy has seen and done it all and in his day hung out with some of the North's most notorious faces, including Paul Sykes.

\*     \*     \*     \*

I first met Paul in Armley Prison I was doing a four stretch along with Delroy Showers from Liverpool and Mick Hartley from Accrington, Burnley. I already knew those guys we'd been criminal associates for some time, but not Paul. That four stretch was the first and only time I'd been to prison. I've been arrested and in the dock a few times, but only sent down the once, in some respects I was lucky compared to the other people I associated with who did a lot more serious time.

Whilst in the nick, Paul was notorious, he did what he wanted, when he wanted, no one could control him. I'll tell you of a few instances of exactly that.

One night in the nick, I could hear absolute bedlam on the landing above, it sounded like a riot, but it was often just Paul on his own, no one could get the screws attention like Paul! He'd picked up the prison bed and was smashing it repeatedly into the door like you wouldn't believe, there is no doubt he would have taken the door off completely before long with his strength. He was doing it in demand for a fresh razor, you could still have them back then, one a week. Anyway, the screws backed down and he got what he wanted, this would never happen with anyone else, but Paul always got what he wanted, not even reprimanded for that kind of behaviour, no one else got away with it.

Another time we were at the servery and Paul would never eat chips, but I'd eat fucking anything. I was behind him in the queue so, he went "Ere give my chips to him", looking out for me, so the screw in defiance put about two chips onto my plate, in the blink of an eye Sykesy grabbed the bloke's wrist and tipped a whole pile of chips on to my plate. The look on the Screw's face. They were all scared of him, cons as well, everyone feared him, he was a handful to say the least. They couldn't get him to his cell unless they were mob handed, they had to wait until he'd calmed down or he wanted to go, but he was the one making the decisions trust me.

Another time I was in Liverpool, down the block on H1. I was in my cell, I was on bread and water then, and they'd even taken my bread off me, so what's that leave I ask you? and we had to live on this! Suddenly, I heard Sykesy, they were bringing him down the block, so what did he do, he walked straight into the governor's office and took his radio back, they wouldn't take it off him, they couldn't even if they wanted to. He took it back to his cell and listened to his usual more intellectual radio programmes such as plays, the cricket and the news, he never listened to music as such like everyone else. Then the next thing I heard, my cell doors opened, they gave me my radio back. He'd demanded we all get our radios back, everyone on the block, rest assured the second he was moved on they took them all straight back, no good bastards!

He was a very clever man, he could do the Telegraph crossword in about twenty minutes, try it, he always exercised his brain, he never wasted a lot of time in the nick, he was always on with learning something. A very underrated man, he just had some queer ways, queer as in strange. If you got on with him he was fine, but if you didn't then woe be tide.

I would also go weight lifting with Paul inside, just to pass time, I was in the weight lifting team at Durham I had a 1.1 snatch, this was at

11 stone 3, and a 210lb clear and jerk, those are Olympic lifting terms. This was nothing compared to Paul who could stand and press 300lb, unbelievably powerful man and he had a lot further to lift these things than me.

When I'd finished my time, I was being released from Durham and who was waiting for me at the gate, but Paul Sykes and Delroy. We headed straight off and stopped off at the Scotch Corner Hotel for some breakfast, strangely enough it was Porridge, like I hadn't had enough, there was a bottle of champagne and a bottle of milk on offer, I went for the milk, it was just what I'd fancied, I'd missed it more inside than the alcohol, or I did at that very moment. From there on Paul was part of our circle and I spent a lot more time in his company. I used to go over to Wakefield quite a lot to see Paul and a few others, usually to discuss some business or spotted opportunities.

I remember I travelled up to John Spensley's Boxing Club to watch Paul fight Mac somebody I think, I don't recall his full name. The Club had a Snooker Hall upstairs. I met all the faces whilst up there, Tommy Harrison etc.

After the bout, we were coming back down the motorway a mob of us and we stopped off at a hotel just off the A1 as we were all desperate for a 'varnish'. We were all in the lobby (the lounge area), Delroy was with us, and Tommy Miller I think. Well, I have a little anecdote from the journey back from there. In the hotel lobby Paul was 'effing and blinding' and this guy stood up and said do you mind not swearing in front of my wife. Paul turned around and said, "This is Great Britain, we have freedom of speech and I will say whatever I want", the guy persisted and eventually offered Paul "Outside", I thought "Fucking hell", as soon as Paul stood up the severity of the situation hit the guy, he hadn't realised what a giant Paul was. Not to lose face they both walked outside. As they were just heading out of the door I turned to the guy's wife and said, "Don't worry, he won't hurt him love, it's alright nothing will happen", a matter of seconds later Sykesy came lumbering back in on his own, the other fella nowhere in sight, he'd only filled him in, in the car park, I turned to his wife again and said, "Sorry I didn't think he would anyway'. We couldn't go anywhere.

Paul used to collect debts for Tommy Miller, I remember one time I went along with him on one of the collections and he went up to the door and said, "Look they've sent me along to try and reason with ya, because next time it'll be the big lads that come!", that was a joke of Pauls, they didn't really come any bigger than him, that wasn't possible. One time, Paul had tipped us off about a wagon full of sugar in Wakefield, sugar! We'd steal anything in those days, but we were known burglars at the time, and away we took it pallet loads of the stuff all labelled up 'A1 Sugar'. Anyway, we took it back to Sheffield and stuck it at the back of Mick Hodge's old place. We didn't know what to do with it, so we ended up taking it back over to Wakefield and parking it outside Mick Seller's shop, Paul brokered the deal with Mick and he bought the lot, lord knows how he shifted it, it could have taken a while through his little Grocery Shop. There was literally enough sugar to last Lupset for a life time.

Another time we were at Paul's sister Kay's gymkhana, she had a little thing for me, but I wasn't interested, I never took to her, it never came to anything. We used to go to these often, me Delroy and sometimes others. This one time one of the horses kicked back. I'm not quite sure if it nearly caught Paul or one of us, but Paul reeled back and hit it just under the jaw full tilt, bang on the money, and it just keeled over. Knocked out a horse, god's honest truth, on my life. I'm sure Kay would confirm it.

Kay his sister was a market trader, our little syndicate would often sell our ill-gotten hauls through her stall in Wakefield, whether she knew it or not I couldn't say, I'd tell the lads don't take the heavy leather goods, expensive gear always took longer to shift. I'd tell the grafters to bring back piles of knickers, boxer shorts, things like that, stuff that would fly out quickly. They made a tidy few quid through the stall that way, like I say I'm not sure they always realised where these things had come from, but it happened. The last time I ever spoke to her she'd rang me to tell me Paul had died.

Paul would often involve me in bits of intimidation, one time I was at a wedding in Rotherham and he'd asked me to come over and do a house over of a witness in an upcoming court case. I'd had to sneak out of the wedding I was at, still togged out in my full velvet suit, I looked the bollocks. We needed to steal a motor for the job so as not to be implicated, so me and Davy Gardner from Newcastle went into town and took one, I remember it still, a ford escort, with plastic seats.

When I got there Paul handed me too big tins of light blue paint he had ready, we took them round to throw all over the inside of someone's house, I did upstairs and my pal did downstairs. Just as we were leaving I looked back through the window to see a big black, now light blue cat, jumping up at the window, it was bizarre as hell. I got back in the car and I had blue paint all over me and the car seats, but I had to return to the wedding. In those days, few people went to the police and if they did then we had to find a way to change their minds.

I also used to head over to Blackpool with Paul, often to see Ronnie Threlfall, one of Blackpool's local faces. I wasn't there but Paul once got done for robbing a bookies over in Blackpool, how he got caught you couldn't make it up. Paul and the other guy involved stole two cars, one to do the job and one to switch further down the road, but what did they steal? Two identical Jags in exactly the same colour, they didn't have the same plates, but that didn't matter they fitted the bill in a near perfect match of a car, that showed you how much they gave a fuck. Might as well have been the same motor full stop for what it mattered in the end.

I went to a lot of Paul's fights, including the one against American Dave Wilson at the Wakefield Theatre Club, Sykesy didn't half give it to him. Wilson was over the ropes and still taking a pummelling, it would have killed most people.

That night Paul was supposed to be having a big party back at the farm house he lived in and I was attending, when I got there my car was well and truly blocked in, this was before the fight, there were that many people there. So, I took Paul's Volvo, I didn't even ask, I had a bird with me and I must not have been used to the car because I ended up blowing the engine up, driving about in second gear, even down the motorway taking this bird back to Sheffield before returning for the fight/party, I blew it to bits, I'd been on the gargle, driving around in drive mode or something. I had to sort it anyway, I can't remember if I got him a new engine or a new car, but I sorted it.

After the American had come out of hospital he went to live at Paul's house until he was well enough to fly home, the old farm house near the stables mentioned in his book, and I'll never forget what came out of Paul's mouth. Austin Mitchell from Calendar was also there at the time. Paul turned to the black guy and said, "Would you have still come over if you'd knew what was going to happen?" Wilson turned to him and said, "You fucking half-wit of course I wouldn't have come" what a question, you never knew if it was just another element to Paul's humour, he was a very intelligent man, trust me.

He said in his book he was a bit reticent thereafter when knocking people about in the boxing ring, but I honestly don't think that would have been the case, Paul knew no bounds. It wouldn't have bothered the Paul that I knew.

I was also at his house for the sham marriage as us lot referred to it, the one on the documentary Paul Sykes at Large. I'd gone on my own, all the faces turned up from all over the country, but I didn't want to be seen amongst them. I kept well away from the cameras, I really didn't want to be seen on camera with some of the Preston lot, I think I had to go to court in a month or so's time to say I didn't even know them, so hopefully you couldn't really see me on there. Most people were getting a little irritated as Paul was blind drunk, it really was a sham, though Cathy was a lovely girl, shame for her.

I went down for the Gardner fight to meet the Richardson's at The Holiday Inn in Chelsea, they were also friends of ours, it was a nice hotel with a swimming pool on the second floor. I ordered a plate of sandwiches, £27 quid! Seriously back then as well, I nearly hit the roof, I'm from Sheffield that made no sense to me. There wasn't room for us to stay in that hotel as it was chocker for the fight. Me and the Mrs borrowed Del's Rolls Royce which was parked outside and went to find somewhere else to stay. I drove around the corner to another hotel in the Roller, pulled up outside and bumped it up on to the kerb, not giving a fuck, completely unlike the average Rolls Royce owner. So, we went into the Hotel and the receptionist said, "First name?" my Mrs said, "Alice second name Cooper" I burst out laughing, we had no chance of getting in now, so we headed off for the next one. I remember it to this day, what a thing to come out with.

We headed back to the Holiday Inn and I went to the room to see Sykesy and Dr McGill was injecting Sykesy with something, I don't know what it was but it was supposed to give him a boost of some sort, but it did the total opposite, it flattened him. I'm not making excuses for him over the fight, I know he hadn't trained hard enough anyway, he was drinking a lot, and was underweight, not the Sykesy who would normally go into battle. He asked me how he looked, I said "You're too skinny, you'll have no power" and that was the case that night, usually when he hit you, you weren't coming back.

In other outrageous incidents, some a little blurry, he once pulled out a birds used Tampax in the pub that he'd managed to get from some tramp and literally ate it with his drink. At home, he also used to piss in the sink in whatever room, and he used to say, "If you can't stand up and piss in the sink you're not a real man", crackers!

I never had a lot to do with Paul during his decline into alcohol, I'd left the country by then, but I knew he liked a drink. No one could control him, not even the prisons, he had his own rules, who could deal with that. I didn't think there was anything really wrong with him, he was clever and he did what he wanted. He was always ok with me. He was a friend to me but no doubt about it he was a handful.

*"If you're not prepared to fight then you shouldn't argue"*

**-P Sykes**

# JOSIE THRELFALL

Delroy Showers told me that one of Paul's closest friends was a man by the name of Ronnie Threlfall. I was aware of the name as I'd already read Sweet Agony and I remembered that Paul's Sister Kay had told me that if I could get hold of Ronnie he would be a minefield of information and would know some stories about Paul.

I asked Delroy if he would kindly get hold of Ronnie's number for me but I didn't hold out much hope particularly as I'd spent a large amount of time trying to contact Ronnie myself.

To my surprise the ever impressive Delroy Showers came up trumps for me but he told me I should really speak to Ronnie's lovely wife Josie first as Ronnie had had some ill health and had not been too well of late. I rang and spoke with both Ronnie and Josie but it was Josie who would tell me about their old friend Paul Sykes.

\*      \*      \*      \*

I'm 65 now and I've been with Ronnie for many years, we're both from Blackpool but we live in Sheffield now.

Many years ago, my Husband Ronnie was extremely close to Paul Sykes, I suppose we both were really but my Ronnie had been great friends with him since the 1960's. He would quite regularly come to Blackpool, he stayed with us for many weekends over the years.

A lot of the stories I used to hear about Paul were very far-fetched I always thought. You were better off making up your own mind about Paul rather than listen to the stories about him and make a judgement from them as what people didn't know they very often just made up about him.

Ronnie met Paul in Walton Prison in 1968 as Ronnie was the barber in there and he cut Paul's hair. Ronnie did six years that time around and spent most of that time with Paul.

Ronnie said one of the things he remembered about Paul was that he would always get his own way regarding the way he wanted things in prison.

To tell the truth the first time I met Paul I thought he was a bit scary and it was only as I got to know him that I found him to be anything but.

Paul would go on to box at the Blackpool Tower in 1978 which is when I really remember him being around a lot at that time.

Paul met his first wife Pauline in Blackpool and he also lived there with his second Wife Wendy in a flat near the Railway Club, so I would say he liked the area. The work he did while around Blackpool was mainly debt collecting but he did work as a Life Guard on the pier for a little while.

Ronnie had Paul and his Mother Betty over to stay in Blackpool at his flat for a weekend and this one evening they didn't have anything in for tea so Paul told Ron to get his wellingtons on and he took him over a field full of cows and when he got to the biggest cow he could see Paul took out this bloody great big hunting knife and slaughtered it there and then. Well Ronnie couldn't believe what he was seeing and he was in total shock. Ron thinks Paul did it because he didn't want it to look like he'd let his Mother down by not being able to feed her while they visited and even though Ron knew it was an oddball thing to do he went along with it to keep the peace and helped Paul carry this big bloody cow home. They got it back and Paul cooked it and made everyone eat the thing but that's just what he was like.

We both thought that there was something wrong with him as he did things that people just don't do normally.

Ronnie used to say that Paul looked up greatly to his friend Delroy Showers and would try to use the same vocabulary that Del did, he looked up to Del even though he was five years older than Del was.

Ronnie, Del and Paul were three very close friends but both Del and Ronnie knew Paul would cross the line many times and sometimes bring embarrassment on them both. This was purely down to Paul doing things that didn't need to be done. Del and Ronnie both loved Paul but I'm sure both would agree, that Paul brought them unwanted attention sometimes when it was needless. By this I mean that they'd be in a club having a nice time and then suddenly 'BANG' Paul has punched someone's lights out and the police and ambulance would be on their way with a dozen witness' staring at them. Despite these scenes sometimes they were close and I know even to this day Ronnie misses Paul like mad.

Tommy Harrison from Middlesbrough used to come through to Blackpool quite a bit too he was also close friends with Paul, Del and Ronnie.

Paul took it really hard when his Son Paul Jnr was convicted of murder in 2004, it absolutely shattered him.

Paul and Wendy had a very turbulent relationship, she was very young when she got with him and Paul would dictate everything to her, she looked up to him but as she got older she knew she didn't want that life and she left Blackpool and Paul to go back home to Wakefield. After that I lost contact with Wendy but she was a lovely girl. When Wendy left Paul, he went back to Cath, again like Wendy another lovely girl but of course they clashed they were in love with the same man.

The time that Paul got married on the TV documentary, I didn't get to that as I wasn't well but Ronnie went with little Teddy Long. When Ronnie came back and told me what had happened I was glad I'd been poorly. You heard what Paul said, "We're married and that's it" and I suppose in his own mind they were.

He was far from a simple man though, he would do the Times crossword and he was very quick, it wouldn't take him very long at all until he had finished it!

A funny memory I have of him is that one of his favourite songs was 'Nutbush City Limits' by Tina Turner and he would get up when it was played and he would shadow box around the place.

I got on well with Paul's little sister Kay, she was lovely. I remember that Ronnie and I went to stay at Paul's parents' house on Gloucester Road in Lupset. I was particularly fond of his Father Walter but Paul didn't treat him very nicely. I remember Walter telling Ronnie "I love him he's my Son but they should do with him what they do with wild dogs and that's shoot him". He said he was no good to anyone and the way he spoke to him was terrible. When Ronnie used to go mad at Paul for having a go at Walter he used to say, "Aye I know I go on at me Dad Ron, but I won't let anyone else say anything bad about him". Paul put both his parents through such a bad time. Can you blame that on his time in prison? I don't know, I mean look at Delroy Showers he's done some serious prison but you could take him anywhere even to Buckingham Palace and he'd be the most eloquent, polite and just the perfect gentleman that you could ever wish to meet. Delroy's manners are impeccable. With Paul Sykes, well he could turn either way it all depended on his mood that day.

Paul in my mind was purely institutionalised and that's why he couldn't cope on the out. The final straw I think for Paul was when Cathy left him. That was when he started hitting the drink badly and he stopped looking after himself, before that I'd always known Paul to be very clean indeed.

After Cath, Paul got a flat on his own and that was the start of his downfall and the start of people using him. This is where the change really started in my opinion this was the start of the wheels falling off and he went from the fearless man he once was to very publicly falling to bits.

Paul ended up a desperate sad case and would often get turned away even by the Police because they were just that sick of him and the commotion he caused on a regular basis. It was around this time that he would turn up at Priests houses looking for help, he was that desperate. I know that the Mental Health Officers had been to visit Paul in his flat and declared it unfit for human habitation.

Paul would often commit crime to end up back in Prison because he preferred that to living on the streets which is what eventually happened to him. Paul spent the last few days of his life living in fear and constantly looking over his shoulder.

At times, he used to turn up drunk in a taxi from Wakefield to our house in Blackpool and I used to feel awful but I used to say to Ronnie "No no Ronnie he can't stay here". This would be when Paul had fallen out with one of his girlfriends and would be in a drunken state. He was just too much of a handful and loud and lairy.

Paul was known to the taxi drivers in Blackpool and I remember one turning up, realising it was for Paul and driving off again.

Another tale was of my Brother in Law, he was working as a taxi driver and he took Paul from Blackpool back to Wakefield. When they arrived, Paul told him he had no money but offered him Cannabis in payment. I think because he was my Brother in Law he got paid in the end but poor Wendy had to go to the bank and sort it out.

Ronnie and Paul would go on to rob a bookies in Hartlepool. Ronnie got four years and Paul got five years. That failed robbery ended up in the News of the World. They got caught because Ronnie and Paul went into a pub and started talking about it. As it happens it turns out that a few off-duty policemen were in the pub that night and they'd overheard the whispers! It didn't help either I suppose that the getaway car that they used had Boxing gloves hanging from the rear-view mirror and Paul was a Boxer, it wasn't the brightest thing to do!

Paul was hard work sometimes and he got himself into plenty of scrapes but he was a character and he is still greatly missed even to this day.

# CHRIS LAMBRIANOU

Many readers, particularly those of you who like a bit of true crime reading, will be familiar already with the name Christopher Lambrianou. Chris was part of the Kray firm for many years and copped a 15yr stretch when the Kray twin's ship sank famously in 1969 at The Old Bailey in Court 1.

Chris and his Brother Tony were both seen as accessories to the murder of Jack 'The Hat' McVitie as they had both been told to fetch him to a house on Evering Road in Stoke Newington. That fateful night Reggie Kray killed Jack and the rest is history!

I spoke to Chris initially with a view to an interview for Unfinished Agony but one way or another we lost touch. I managed to get back in touch with him via my publishers Warcry Press. On speaking with Chris, I could tell immediately that he was very fond of his old friend Paul Sykes and that he had known him well, after all, Chris had lived on the same landing as Paul in Hull Prison for over three years.

\*      \*      \*      \*

I had never heard of Paul Sykes until I went to Hull Prison in the early 1970's. I was a category A man so I was moved around the dispersal system and this is how I ended up in Hull with a friend of mine called Freddie Sansom, he was the cousin of the former England and Arsenal footballer Kenny Sansom. We'd both been in a riot at Albany Prison so they kicked us out of there and sent us both to Hull. When I arrived at Hull all the screws had been briefed to be strict as they didn't want the Kray firm taking over. On getting there they didn't want to give me my shaving stuff, hair gel and toothpaste that kind of thing, so I started to kick off anyway I go on the wing and Charlie Kray was there and one of the Train Robbers Bobby Walsh came at me saying "Chris just let it go until the morning" but I was so pissed off that one of the Screws came and said, "Here take this, you'll be alright" and gave me a little tablet. Within one minute of taking what it was he gave me I was out like a bloody light. So, I wake up in the morning and I went out onto the landing and Charlie Kray says to me "Chris please I just wanna get out I wanna get parole don't get me into anything" by that he means that he didn't want to be getting into any riots or anything like that. They moved me onto another wing called B Wing after that.

I knew that a good friend of mine was already in there he had been arrested with me in May 1968 and his name was Ronnie Bender. Ronnie was doing twenty to life and he was the one that introduced me to this guy called Paul Sykes.

I'll be honest with you, the Paul Sykes I knew didn't trust anybody. So, if you watch Paul Sykes at Large he does say that he respected myself, my brother Tony, Ronnie Bender, Freddie Mills and the Train Robbers. These were all people that were coming and going, they were getting moved around the system.

Paul wanted to be his own man and he certainly didn't want anyone using him so he would often come across quite fierce and he'd push people away, I got the impression from him that the only people he did trust were the Cat A men doing a long time, the ones that had been through the mill and had been what he'd been through.

The general consensus among your ordinary folk was that Paul was this wicked dangerous man but he wasn't always like that, Paul had a softer side to him massively, now I'm not talking about him being a softy I'm saying he was a man with a heart. Something else I'll add is that he wasn't frightened of anyone, I'll give him that.

When Paul was in Hull he was a supremely super fit guy and he would love to get in the ring in the gym and have a jump about. I remember the time Ronnie Bender said to me "Chris, Paul's brilliant I'm gonna get in touch with Alex Steen". Ronnie did just that for Paul and Alex Steen came up to Hull Prison with a couple of other chaps. They spoke with Paul Sykes and they must have thought he had something as they got Floyd Patterson's brother Ray to spar with Paul. I'll tell you now, because I was there and witnessed it, Paul held his own with the then experienced Heavyweight Ray Patterson, no problem whatsoever. He also did a bit of sparring with the Hull Heavyweight Roger Tighe, Paul was bloody good!

We were friends and we used to chat, he was a very clever man you know. He very much reminded me of my friend Charlie Richardson who was also really well read. Charlie would give people a book and then quiz them about it to check they'd read it. Paul Sykes was the same, read digest it, read digest it, Paul took in every word. Quite often Paul would read books and he'd get other prisoners interested in it because he would talk about it. He just did so much reading. In all my 15 years of being in prison I never met anyone who studied like Paul Sykes did.

At that time in Hull we had a go at the authority and I tell you what, Paul Sykes was right there with us. On one occasion, all the guys on the wing wanted to watch the Olympic Games so when it came time for them to lock us back up we wouldn't let them, this was the whole of the prison, Paul was the ringleader if you like and he got his own way in the end. I remember that night sat watching the boxing with big Paul. Paul was desperate to watch the British Middleweight Alan Minter and the Welterweight Maurice Hope. Paul would of course go on to fight on the same show as Alan Minter when he faced John L Gardner.

Paul loved boxing and had been clean living, he was one hell of a lump, when he got in the gym he really worked hard.

I always followed Paul's boxing career and I thought he could have beaten Gardner and if it had been the Paul Sykes of 1972 I think he may well have done but of course he just turned over a bit too late to give himself a fair chance at it.

It's a shame I never got to see Paul outside of prison. He was from the North and we were from the South and to be quite truthful when I left prison I put it all behind me, all I wanted to do was forget about prison but I always thought of Paul over the years and wondered how he was doing and how he was getting on.

Paul was never a bully in my company he wouldn't bully anyone. Truth is he didn't need to, all he had to do was put his shadow over someone and they'd walk away. One of his favourite sayings was that he didn't like liberty takers and if he had something he wanted to say to you he didn't have to say an awful lot put it that way. No one was ever in a hurry to have a row with Paul Sykes let me tell you and I find all the rumours about Paul Sykes and young lads absolutely bloody bollocks, if that had been going on he wouldn't have walked with us.

Paul lived by his own set of rules and he didn't stand for any bloody nonsense if he felt he had to say something he'd say it in the plainest terms, if you were a cunt he'd tell you that you were a cunt you understand.

Paul Sykes never gave anyone any grief that way no one would give him grief, that is the golden rule in prison if you've got things going your way then why fuck it up.

If I could sum up my old friend Paul in one sentence I'd say he was tough but fair. I was very sad to hear of how Paul finished his life, very sad. He finished his life on the floor and most things said about him were not very nice.

God will one day judge the people who pushed a defenceless man into that situation. People who gave him booze when he shouldn't have had it people who gave him drugs when he shouldn't have had it them people will all stand condemned one day. It's all a crying shame.

There's a very famous poem by Maya Angelou and it's called "I know why a caged bird sings" and I'd like to add this please about Paul, this for me sums him up.

# I KNOW WHY A CAGED BIRD SINGS
## Maya Angelou

*The free bird leaps*
*On the back of the wind*
*And floats downstream*
*Till the current ends*
*And dips his wings*
*In the orange sun rays*
*And dares to claim the sky.*

*But a bird that stalks*
*Down his narrow cage*
*Can seldom see through*
*His bars of rage*
*His wings are clipped and*
*His feet are tied*
*So, he opens his throat to sing.*

*The caged bird sings*
*With fearful trill*
*Of the things unknown*
*But longed for still*
*And his tune is heard*
*On the distant hill for the caged bird*
*Sings of freedom.*

*The free bird thinks of another breeze*
*And the trade winds soft through the sighing*
*Trees*
*And the fat worms waiting on a dawn-bright lawn*
*And he names the sky his own.*

*But a caged bird stands on the grave of dreams*
*His shadow shouts on a nightmare scream*
*His wings are clipped and his feet are tied*
*So, he opens his throat to sing*

*The caged bird sings*
*With a fearful trill*
*Of things unknown*
*But longed for still*
*And his tune is heard*
*On the distant hill*
*For the caged bird*
*Sings of freedom.*

That poem for me is Paul Sykes. He never ever got out of his cage throughout the whole of his life. You don't come out of prison the same and even when you come out you're still in prison. Sometimes I think I wouldn't mind going back in a cell because I could be myself, I had time to read and time to write. Now I'm running at 100 mile an hour, I've got a large family, a house to run, got a nice car, now I've got everything a man could ask for. I've got a lot of love in my life these days.

Paul Sykes wanted to go down another road, get the anger out and fight. Paul Sykes back in his day reminded me of a Centurion that went out with a sword. He was just born at the wrong time he should have been a Gladiator fighting lions for a living.

Paul Sykes never left prison, even when he was out he took it with him, he took his cage with him. It's just all very sad because he had so much going for him. The man I knew in prison was something else and I'm just sad he never filled his potential in his life. I'm so sorry Paul R.I.P my old friend.

I feel like I need to add something about my good friend Ronnie Bender, he was a real champion of Paul Sykes' he really believed in Paul Sykes and wanted Paul to better himself, Paul liked Ronnie Bender because he was a strong man, they were very close, after all it was the call by Ronnie to Alex Steen that got Paul's boxing career started. Unfortunately, Ronnie passed away about seven years ago now after a heart attack. He was one of those people though that thought of other people, you must remember now that Ronnie Bender didn't murder anyone, he was left by the Kray Twins to clean up after Reggie had murdered Jack 'The Hat' McVitie, but when he was stood in the dock in the Old Bailey, he was making jokes trying to keep everyone else's spirits up and that's what got him 20 years instead of the 15 like my brother and I did! They just thought he wasn't showing any remorse.

He was a great sportsman, whatever he turned his hand to, football, snooker it didn't matter what it was he was good at it. When he got out he was involved in kid's football. Overall, he was just a good guy, strong and he had a great sense of humour. He is missed. - Chris.

*"I'd rather be the local drunk then the local fucking nowt. Nowts are born like the mayfly. They're born, they grow up, they mate, and they die in a day"*

**-P Sykes**

# HARRY LAKES

You may remember from Sykes – Unfinished Agony that Kevin Kilty mentions Harry Lake in his interview and it was clear from speaking to Kevin that Harry was someone Kevin had looked up to as a lad and someone who he still speaks highly of now. Kevin had said that Harry was a real hard man in his youth who could really look after himself.

Harry had been in and out of Jail like Paul Sykes but he's been a scaffolder for the past 40 years. I managed to get hold of Harry and thankfully he agreed to be interviewed.

\*　　　\*　　　\*　　　\*

The first time I clapped eyes on Paul was in Durham Prison in 1974, I was doing two years at the time and Paul was doing his time for the bookies robbery in Hartlepool and, as it happens, he was kicking off!

We were all lining up for breakfast and Paul didn't like being told what to do at the best of times, he had a major dislike for authority of any kind so when a screw came up to him while he was laughing and joking and said to Paul "oi you shut it" Paul didn't take kindly to it. Lightening quick he turned around and belted this screw knocking him clean out! Paul hit a couple of screws that morning and I mean he put them to sleep out cold on the floor.

After a few minutes of all hell breaking loose the screws managed to overpower Paul but it took about a dozen of them to hold him down. Paul was taken down the Chokey and we were all locked up back in our cells with no breakfast!

I used to see Paul regularly on the exercise yard and I used to think he consistently looked like he was drugged up with liquid cosh. There's actually no doubt in my mind that this was what Paul was on as they used to dish it out back then. I've had it myself so I know what the effects are and how it makes a person act. When Paul used to be speaking he was slurring a lot and would be very pale. Normally, Paul would have a brisk sort of walk and usually would walk with his hands behind his back but when he was drugged up you'd see him moving around the yard in slow motion and I've no doubt that it was because he was kept drugged up 90 percent of the time.

The whole of the prison system was completely terrified of him I can tell you that! He was such a big powerful man who really had his wits about him and a normal functioning Paul Sykes was a complete nightmare to control so they kept him pumped up with this stuff that made him vacant at best, so that made their job a lot easier didn't it.

Myself, personally I never had a problem with Paul and he always treat me with respect. Although you couldn't ever relax around him you always had to be on your guard, well you had to be after hearing all the stories about Paul, anyone would have been on edge around him.

That morning when I saw Paul fighting with all the screws I realised that this man was no fucking mug, far from it. Paul Sykes was a fucking big fine fella and he always looked after himself to the very highest standard. He followed a strict training regime and training was Paul's life while he was in there I can tell you and even though we were in prison he wouldn't eat shite. He used to insist on better food and if truth be told he got what he wanted! The screws used to give him what he wanted just to keep him quiet. Paul Sykes was the top man in Durham prison in my time there for sure.

Another thing I'd like to say is Paul Sykes never raped anyone in there. He did have sex with a few gadgies in there but rape, absolutely not. I used to see the young lads going in his cell and hanging around with Paul to get in his good books. It was obvious they were going in to give Paul sexual favours but there was never any rape, not in my time in Durham with him anyway.

The pictures I've seen of Paul looking like the alcoholic tramp he became utterly amaze me I tell ya! When I first saw them, I didn't believe that it was Paul Sykes because he was the cleanest living man you could ever meet in 1974. I was also amazed to hear the stories about him being beaten up because he just wouldn't have tolerated that kind of shit. The man wasn't to be crossed in his prime.

I was aware of Paul coming to my hometown of Middlesbrough in later years, he was here quite regularly. I never saw him in Boro though as I was either working away or locked up whilst he was in my town.

Paul frequented the Spensley's pub when he was in town and I know he was hired by a few fella's, I won't mention names, for debt collecting purposes in Middlesbrough. If you wanted to hire him though he was extremely reliable and when he took a job he got it done, he didn't give a fuck about anyone. I'm just so shocked that Paul Sykes' life ended up the way it did!

# REG LONG

Reg Long is 66 now and lives in Middlesbrough. Reg was one of the first people I interviewed for this book as initially I was going to put him in Unfinished Agony but I had only managed to interview him by phone and I really wanted to meet Reg in person so we could speak properly. We arranged to meet in The Dickens Inn in Middlesbrough which is one of the pubs owned by Paul's mentor John Spensley.

*       *       *       *

I'm now a Steward for the British Boxing Board of Control but in my youth, many years ago, I boxed professionally in the late 1970's and early 80's. I won the Northern Area Light Heavyweight title and I also fought for the Northern Area Heavyweight title but didn't win as I was beaten by George Scott. George Scott was mentioned in Sweet Agony as he was the boxer that Paul travelled to Middlesbrough to spar with in 1977. I had a career that lasted six years, winning nine, losing seventeen and drawing twice.

I fought Neil Malpass as an amateur and he was a powerful man who could really hit with the right hand. Neil went on to have a decent career as a pro himself.

One of the highlights of my boxing career was being able to have a sparring exhibition with the greatest, Muhammad Ali! I went in and did a few rounds with Ali after Richard Dunne when Ali came to South Shields in 1977. It was like sparring with Jesus Christ!

I enjoyed my time in boxing and when age caught up with me I started working in the game outside of the ropes.

The first time I heard the name Paul Sykes was when I was told he sparred with the great Joe Frazier down at the Thomas A Beckett Gym in 1973. Joe Frazier was here to fight Joe Bugner and he needed a big hard punching heavyweight to mimic Bugner so that's why big Paul got the shout to go down to London.

Sykesy did very well sparring Joe and won a lot of praise from Frazier but he didn't half take some lumps and bumps from Frazier's left hook because it was like being hit by a train! Paul took it and did well in the camp and it was a great experience for him. Paul was 27 at the time and that would have been an appropriate time for him to go pro but of course Paul was knocked back, refused a licence and ended up back inside for a few years after that. That was the time he robbed the bookies in Hartlepool and he got five years for it.

The reason he got caught for it was that he used his own car and parked it right outside instead of around the corner and of course it didn't help that his rear-view mirror had a pair of boxing gloves hanging from it, bit of a giveaway to say the least!

Paul did, for some strange reason, get granted a BBBofC Licence in 1978 when he was past his best. I don't understand why he was knocked back in 1973 then was granted one after he had done more prison, it was bizarre! I think John Spensley and Tommy Miller were largely responsible for him being granted one at the second time of asking.

I think Paul Sykes at 21 could have really done something in the boxing world, for me Paul certainly could have set the European scene alight. Of course, I'd heard of all the stigma that Paul's name carried with it but there was boxing stories connected to his name also. For instance, the lad Paul Tucker who beat me in the ABA's went on to face Paul Sykes in the next round and Sykes beat him easily on a wide points decision. Paul was then beaten in the semis by a lad from Birmingham called Garfield McEwan and McEwan went on to win it by beating Neville Meade in the final of 1973.

The first time I ever met Paul Sykes was up in Radio Taxis when John Spensley had the gym at the back of his Taxi firm, this was in '77.

I think the reason Paul was up was to spar with big George Scott who'd just gone professional.

My first thought on Paul Sykes was that he was a large imposing man. I myself was 6ft 1 and 12st 7 and Paul was 6ft 3 and 15st 7 but very, very strong.

I sparred a couple of rounds that night and with me being a light heavyweight I thought I'd be too quick for him, nobody could run backwards faster than I could and when I had a fella like Paul Sykes in front of me I had to! Looking at Paul stripped off in 1978 you could see he was an awesome specimen let me tell you from first-hand experience.

To give you an example of how strong he was, I bounced a big right hand off him and he didn't even blink. It was a pearler of a shot but he just looked at me as if to say, 'well you're going to pay for that' then he backed me onto the ropes and really let the leather swing at me. I was a very quick fighter though so I got on my bike and away from Paul, I banged another flush on his face, he chased me again and I was thinking that if he got me in the corner this time that he was going to kill me but to be quite truthful, Paul never fully opened up on me. Paul knew he was levels above me and never took any liberties with me in sparring. Paul let me know who was the boss though!

John and George Feeney from Hartlepool trained at that gym along with Stewart Lithgo, Maxie Smith and Neil Malpass joined us at the end of that year also after he fought Paul.

I knew Paul was a level above me physically and technically. Paul just moved me around most sessions and went through the motions, he knew I was a lot smaller so he never took advantage.

I saw Paul sparring with George Scott and with Scotty being 17st 7lbs I watched some good tear ups between them two. To give you some idea on just how strong Sykesy was, he had big Scotty in the corner, both were really letting their shots go with great ferociousness and suddenly Sykes just stopped, grabbed hold of big Scotty and physically just picked him up, walked him to the opposite corner of the ring and said, "I'm tired of hitting you in that corner, I'm going to hit you in this corner now" and that was a 17 plus stone man he did that with. George Scott gave as good as he got though, and they were very entertaining to watch.

Outside of the ring I had a beer with Paul sometimes and I always found him good company. He was clever, witty, sharp and good fun to be around. We'd go in The Boro Hotel just near John Spensley's gym after training, it's called Doctor Browns now. Paul was never a big drinker in them days and I don't think I saw him have any more than two pints and I never saw him behaving inappropriately at all, although he did have an eye for younger girls.

I was boxing in Newcastle at the City Hall against Roy Gregory and Paul Sykes turned up in a big Vauxhall Cresta and it must have been about 20 years old, I remember thinking 'bloody hell where have you got that thing from?' and he had a young girl with him on his arm. I said to him "Paul she's only about 15 or 16" he said, "Reg I've been locked up for 13 years I'm only 15 or 16 myself in my own head". These days he'd be locked up doing that. Paul Sykes never seemed fazed by anything and was always good for a laugh and a joke, always very smart casual and looked after his appearance.

I saw many of Paul's pro fights and my opinion of his fight with John L Gardner is that Paul had left it all in the gym. Paul had trained down to the bone for it. For that fight Paul wasn't even 15st and I thought he looked too light and very skinny. Paul over trained and I feel he lost a lot of his power. At his best, he would weigh 15 stone 7lbs so I can still not understand why he came in at 14st 12lbs. When I'd seen Paul box in the past he had been solid but John L Gardner just seemed to climb through him and Paul had left it all behind in the gym like I said. That's the way I saw it anyway. Paul Sykes certainly had the boxing skills but the fact of the matter was that he was allowed his boxing licence too late to make his mark in the game turning pro when he was 30.

Paul was always nice to me and if I think of Paul Sykes I always think of the day I nearly broke my hand on his face and he looked at me as if to say, 'you better take up draughts Son!'

# DAVE OWENS

Dave Owens is an Ex Professional Middleweight fighter from Castleford, West Yorkshire. Dave had 61 contests over a period from May 1976 to June 1995.

I managed to get in touch with Dave regarding his sparring partner Paul Sykes through his Son Nathan who himself is a lovely guy. I got hold of Nathan through Facebook and dropped him a message to ask if it would be ok to speak to his Father and he told me it was, incidentally Nathan is also an amateur boxer. I couldn't help but see the similarities between Dave and Paul, they had a look of each other, both had moustaches and were two big, dark haired Yorkshire men who boxed.

Before I get to what Dave had to say about Paul, I'd like to remind you all of what Paul says about Dave Owens in his book Sweet Agony.

"When I'd been living with Elaine he'd (Tommy Miller) asked if I would make sure Dave Owens turned up at some big posh hotel on the Ring way in Birmingham, one Sunday morning so he could defend his Central Area Middleweight title. He'd promised to pay me expenses then but he'd conveniently forgotten. It didn't matter and I'd have taken him without any inducements anyway. Dave was my main sparring partner and one of the best boxers I'd ever met.

The gym where I was training was at the Wakefield side of the bus station in Castleford; the gym where Tommy's mate, Burt Corris, the feller who was standing me bail, had a big say in how things were run, and had Dave Owens as the star man. Dave, in my opinion, had the built-in potential to be the World Champion. He was 6ft tall, strong, young and could punch harder than most heavyweights, but his greatest asset was that he thought like a fighter. He waited, moved and exploited the slightest of chinks in any opponent's defence with the silky, smooth precision of a natural champion. Richard Dunne had been to the gym, training to fight Jerrie Coetzee and I'd sparred a few rounds with him but he wasn't in the same league as Dave. Half a dozen times I'd been in the shower when I'd heard my brain crackle as it shook off the effects of Dave's punching and couldn't remember being hit. He was that good he could knock people out without them knowing."

\*       \*       \*       \*

When I was training in the Lumb's gym in Castleford they were suggesting a few names for me to spar with and Paul was one of those.

The things that I'd heard was stuff like Paul was always getting into bother usually when he'd been drinking, but most people liked Paul and I was one of them, he was a good-hearted bloke. As soon as I met Paul I thought he was a cracking bloke and he loved to be the centre of attention telling tales and laughing and joking.

Only tale I can remember is of being pulled aside by Paul in the gym after sparring and him saying "Dave come here I've got summat to show ya" he was excited and giddy as we were walking to his car, he then popped his boot open to reveal a loaded crossbow, I laughed nervously then said, "fuck me Sykesy what's tha goin to do wi that?" he said "I've got a copper in mind, come on Dave lad I'll drop thi back home".

I was never out of my depth sparring Paul and I could quite easily handle the sessions as I was on an unbeaten streak and didn't have any personal problems going on so I was flying as a Pro at that time. Paul was great to spar with as I didn't have to hold back and he didn't either, I used to love going to the gym knowing I would be sparring with Sykesy as I would be able to get some good sparring in.

I would rate Paul definitely in the top 5 in Britain, I thought Paul was big, strong and athletic but was more of a fighter then a neat boxer. I'd always got on with Paul since the first time we met in Lumb's Gym, he was a kind-hearted bloke but could be a swine too. I still have a lot of fond memories about Paul and I wish he was still here now.

# NEIL ATKINSON

My favourite person from Wakefield, Chris Campbell, suggested Neil Atkinson to me.

Neil grew up on the Lupset Estate and is 56 years old now. For many years he worked alongside Chris on the doors of Wakefield's nightclubs. Neil still resides in Lupset to this day.

*    *    *    *

I must have been all of 13/14 when I first remember hearing about Paul Sykes as most of my school friends looked up to him as some sort of hero. My first memory of seeing him was when he used to jog around the estates while he was training for his boxing. Quite often if we were having a game of rugby and Paul was jogging past he would stop running and have a game with us, encourage us all and do a bit of coaching. He was good like that, if he saw anyone doing any training he would be straight over to help.

Paul was as fit as a flea in them days and he loved talking to kids, I think it's because basically he was just a big kid himself. One thing I will say about him is that he always made time for us kids, he wouldn't ever go past without giving us the time of day. We'd see him running up Dewsbury Road daily and many of my mates used to try running with him but none of them could keep up with him as he would always be going at some pace, it was like that scene out of Rocky, all the kids following him running up the road.

Our estate, the Lupset Estate, has always had a bad name so it was a bit of a novelty that we had someone from Lupset who was always on the telly and in the papers so we were all proud of him.

As a lad, I would go to the White Rose Boxing Club and I'd often see him in there giving a hand and he would come over and teach me a few things.

Many years later after Paul had been given his first ASBO that barred him out of Wakefield he would go drinking in Dewsbury where I was working the doors at the time. He would come in the Duke of Wellington in Dewsbury and he came in one day whilst I was on shift. Obviously, the landlady had heard about Paul Sykes and didn't want him in there. So, the landlady says to me "If you get him out I'll pay you double and your drinks are free". This landlady didn't know I knew Paul so I wasn't going to tell her. So, I asked the barmaid to ring a taxi, went over to Paul and said, "Come on mate you've blown it over here you're not welcome". He stood up shook my hand and I took him to his taxi and he went peacefully, well relatively peacefully as when I put him in the back of the taxi and closed the door I could see Paul slapping the taxi driver on the back of the head telling him to drive!

Something I quickly learnt with Paul is that if you tried to confront him, he would stand his ground, but if you treat him respectfully like a fellow human being then you didn't get any confrontation with him. It's the people that thought they were better than Paul and those that tried to treat him like crap that got all the bother from him.

Paul ended up drinking in The Black Bull in Dewsbury which was another down and out place and I think that was one of the only places that would have him in their pub in the end. Most of the patrons in that pub at the time didn't know what day of the week it was and Paul would inevitably end up fighting in there from time to time. One of the things I heard was that he used to fight people in there for a pint of beer, that's how low he'd become.

I never in my entire life had any problems with Paul and that was down to me treating him with respect in my opinion. In fact, one night he helped me out a great deal. One Saturday night on the door in Wakefield I had to kick these two lads out, the next night I was out for a quiet drink with my Wife minding our own business in the Black Bull at the top of Westgate when these two from the night before came up challenging me "Not so hard in your dickie bow now are ya" they were taunting me with. I don't know why they thought it was personal but I'd heard this many times over the years, an argument started and at that moment Paul Sykes and a mate of his walked in "Ey up Neil you having problems lad?" he asked, "Just these two here Paul because I threw them out of the club last night" I said to him, he looked at my Wife "In here with your lass are ya, go get yerself a drink lad I'll deal with this", so off I went around the bar with my Wife. Paul was true to his word he dealt with it alright as ten minutes later I heard an ambulance arrive.

If you got on with Paul and treat him right he would do anything for you, he wouldn't ever be rude if I was with the Wife either, wouldn't swear in front of her he acted the perfect gentleman.

At the back end of Paul's life, you could see he was brain damaged most likely through his alcoholism, his eyes would be vacant and I was disgusted to hear how his life had ended up like that. Even then though, when he was pissed up, I never had a problem with him, he would stagger up and shake my hand when he saw me.

Towards the end of his life something I heard quite a bit was some young buck or another bragging that they'd beaten Paul Sykes in a fight, well no they hadn't none of them had, they never fought Paul Sykes, that man was long gone by then. There was a lot of people that would take the micky out of him and one of the worst ones was Dennis Flint! Dennis just used him. Dennis used to have Waldorf Garage and Paul was forever chasing clients that owed Dennis money. Dennis ended his days on his boat in the sunshine, it was the drink that got him in the end as well.

Sometimes when I used to talk to Paul I'd forget he was a boxer as it would be like talking to a uni lecturer. The brains of that man were frightening and it was never guess work, he really knew what he was on about, whatever subject it was that you wanted to talk about he knew something about it. I could sit and talk to Paul for hours and I often did when I was at college. When he'd had a drink though it was different, you could see that he didn't have the same concentration and he'd wander off.

Paul used to attract the ladies but they were mostly always pretty rough ones, ones that just wanted to say that they'd been with Paul Sykes, many would go and hang around him in the bars, they soon put some distance between themselves and Paul though when he got drunk!

Paul told me loads of tales of how he had made a living going all over the country selling brass as gold, he'd sell gold chains and the next day it would turn their necks green, he knew that there weren't many people that would go and ask for their money back.

Paul lasted longer on this earth than anyone thought he would have done, the only good part of his decline for me as I see it was that when he did die he died in hospital rather than on the street or under a bush.

The last time I saw him it brought a tear to my eye, he was hunched over while walking in the street and he looked destroyed. It was a combination of different things, how he'd led his life and the drink. He lived a full life, short but a lot packed into it and he was burnt out at only 60. He told me once that he only drank to numb his pain.

They'll never be another Paul Sykes. If you've never heard of him then you're not from Wakefield. Some people saw the good side of him and those that saw the bad side of him had upset him in one way or another. There was most likely a genuine reason as to why he was upset with you because a lot of people tried to take the piss out of Paul, he wouldn't have it and would kick back against it. He was just a bit bigger and much more powerful than most, it wasn't his fault he just didn't suffer fools gladly and nobody should. He took it a bit too far at times but Paul had no off button once he got going.

When Paul died I was sad but I was glad also that he wasn't suffering anymore, he was free at last!

All the old school police in Wakefield respected him, they didn't like what he did but they kind of liked him in a strange way. They knew Paul called a spade a spade.

*"I've read 4 books a week for 35 years, been through the classics and back – let's face it, I've had plenty of time and I've read some right trash. The ones I keep coming back to are JB Priestly, AJ Cronin, Delderfield. I don't want to get wealthy writing like Jeffrey Archer. I keep the wolf from the door debt collecting and I want my book to sell so that people will read it"*

**-P Sykes**

# JANET SELLERS

Wife of Mick Sellers RIP

Mick's wife, who was one of the key characters from the book Sweet Agony and beloved Father/Husband to Janet and her kids came over to the publisher's office on the 26th June 2017, along with her youngest Son Mark Sellers, also in the book.

Here's a quick re-cap from Paul's book Sweet Agony regarding his old pal Big Mick Sellers:

The Monday morning, before I could get to a solicitor, I'd been arrested, charged, and remanded in custody for 7 days. The police objected to bail on the grounds the plaintiff, his wife and children were living in constant terror of me, and, of course my record. After 7 days, they used exactly the same excuse and this time the old feller was in court. He went straight to the police complaints department and made a complaint. The copper who'd objected to bail had committed perjury, he'd told deliberate lies under oath and to prove it Mick came to visit the following week.

He had a thick crepe bandage over the injury but even that was hardly noticeable under his thick mat of black hair. His ear would be completely covered. Anyway, he had ears like an elephant and I knew I hadn't ripped it all off, just sort of trimmed it a bit. Smartened it up. Might do the other one if he doesn't get me out I thought, watching him enter the visiting room looking sheepish and embarrassed, and telling me he was sorry. Old Mick would do his level best to get me out but I was up against the coppers and they wanted me away, even Mick knew that now. He wouldn't listen when I'd told him what would happen if he didn't let me take him to the hospital.

'They'll send for the police Mick, once they see what's wrong with you and I'll get five years.' 'No you won't,' he'd promised, 'cos I'll tell 'em the fuckin' dog did it.' He added, 'Now fuck off afore I get the crossbow.' The police were involved up to their necks in the case, doing everything in their power to get Mick to alter his story, and the power they had had frightened him to death. Full-time police protection and all his visitors screened. They'd even stopped his dad from seeing him while he'd been in the hospital but they hadn't hustled him into a little room to see if they could dig something up about me like they'd done with the others.

They'd even been having a go at me through Paul while I'd been serving the last sentence, the old feller had told me. Until then he'd been pro-police. Little Paul, who'd been 21 months old, had been taken into the intensive care unit at Pinderfields after somebody had battered him. That was the diagnosis. Pauline, his mother, blamed her younger brother who'd been baby-sitting but the old feller strongly suspected Pauline. He'd gone up to Wood Street to report it and when the sergeant behind the desk realised I was his father he'd laughed in the old feller's face and asked when I was due to be released. If Mick knew about that little episode he'd realise the powers of the police were unlimited and they could do exactly what they wanted.

Mick gave me plenty to think about before I came up for bail for the third and final time. If it wasn't granted this time I was bang in trouble and the police would be objecting in the strongest possible terms. They'd been objecting since the second week I'd been out of Durham, when one accused me of knocking his elbow in Heppy's. He'd come to the table where I'd been sitting with Patsy and Lily, the two Liverpool girls, and asked if I was looking for a fight because I'd spilt beer all down his sleeve.

Both sleeves were dry and I'd not been near him. Leaning against the bar were five of his oppos supposed to be looking for the Ripper. Without a doubt, I could have battered the lot of the useless bastards but that's what they were after. A week later the same copper came to the house with a sergeant and an inspector to ask why I'd been to the Empire stores last week. This week they'd laid on an armed ambush. They thought I'd been going to rob the wages.

I'd explained I'd been driving past at dinner time just as all the girls were going back in, my pal thought they all looked like American majorettes and wanted to see them again. It was Michael, Del's brother, so I told the manager he was the Nigerian Postmaster-General and we wanted a look round because maybe the company could expand into Africa. We'd been given a conducted tour wearing security badges and seen a dozen girls I knew. They knew we weren't who we said we were and told the gaffer, who in turn told the coppers. They came to the house the day after the ambush wanting to know what my game was and to lay down the law, an inspector, a sergeant, and the copper who'd pulled me in Heppy's. In no uncertain manner, I'd been told if I didn't get off their patch I'd spend 6 months out of every 12 on remand if I did anything or not. The inspector had told Mick while he'd been in hospital and added I shouldn't really be in prison, an animal like me should have my arms off at the elbow and my legs off at the knees and then be released.

The coppers in charge of this case were the sergeant and the one who'd pulled me in Heppy's. Mick said his name was Dawson, and he'd been about Wakefield years. Mick also told me Tommy had been to see him and promised free tickets to my first fight and said this bit of bother wouldn't alter anything, I'd still be on the first bill in the new season.

Tommy was very confident I'd be given bail and even arranged to have the ex-mayor of Castleford stand surety for me. My finger was almost better and I'd regained all the fitness I'd lost with late nights and whizzing about, with regular sleep and a session in the gym every day. Tommy had seen me perform in the ring with Phil Martin, his light-heavy who'd fought weeks earlier for the British title, and Peter. Tommy knew a good thing when he saw it and he had the pull to swing it for me.

Leeds produced me at the Magistrates court for the third time and it all went the prosecution's way until Mick breezed down the aisle and took the oath. When he'd finished the coppers didn't have a case but the old feller did with his complaint. Bail was granted providing I had two sureties of £200 each. The old feller and Burt Corris, Tommy's mate, the ex-Mayor, stood for me and I was released with the only condition being I hadn't to associate with Mick, and to keep away from his shop.

The condition didn't say Mick couldn't associate with me though but apart from buying a car I saw nothing of him, because I was living at the other side of town with Elaine, in her lovely big 3-storey house overlooking the Grammar School playing-field. We spent the first night in the old feller's bed while he'd slept in mine, which had been a real surprise; I'd never thought they'd let me sleep at home with a married woman, and then I'd moved in with Elaine the following day.

Initially Janet was reluctant to give an interview for this book. She'd chosen to put all the episodes involving Paul behind her, for a time he had made life hell for her and her family, but ultimately those problems had made her stronger and in all honesty giving the interview felt like she'd got something off her chest, those were her words.

*  *  *  *

Michael Sellers was born in Flanshaw and I was from Heath Common, we were childhood sweet-hearts, if he hadn't passed away I'm sure I would still be with him to this day. Aside from the stories that follow involving Paul, I'd like to clarify the reality behind the stories involving me, my husband Michael and Paul leading up to the incident in which Paul bit Michaels ear off, and how it differs from what is written in Paul's book Sweet Agony. Paul put things in that book to appease his own failings, there is truth in there but there is also fantasy. Paul could never be wrong not even in his book.

Categorically I can say I was never sweet on him, in fact I never really liked Paul's imposing presence from the off, but he was Michael's long-time friend. Also, when it came to the ear biting incident, I did not retract my statement as an honourable decision for an old friend, I literally feared for mine but more importantly my children's safety, that was the reason I couldn't see it through. I'll tell you more of that and what went off in the paragraphs that follow.

Initially I knew of Paul as an old school friend of my husband Michael's, or as you may know him 'Mick' or locally often referred to as Suggsy Sellers. Paul was a year older than me, I was born 11th May 1947, him one year before on the 23rd May 1946. I'd seen Paul around,

52

and knew of him but he hadn't had much bearing on my life at that point. I barely knew him at all, but I knew he had a bad reputation and he did what he wanted, full stop. He'd batter anyone, young kids you name it, he was not someone I cared for being around me and my family.

He came from a very strange family. His father was, for want of a better term 'tapped' and his mother was more like a bloke, she used to batter Paul with full bottles of lemonade it was all real La-La land stuff. I heard Paul once tied his old man up and left him under the bed for two days, that tells you something doesn't it, he just didn't care, that's not the happenings of a normal family.

The first time I'd had much to do with him was not long after we'd bought the shop at Lupset, the one mentioned in Sweet Agony, it was called 'Janet's Groceries' for obvious reasons. That's where a lot of my recollections of Paul occurred. Not long after we'd taken on the shop he started to turn up, like a Magpie to silver. He first turned up with Michael and they went in to the back and it was simple pleasantries. Then he'd turn up again, and again, but there would be different people with him each time, I was busy running the shop but I knew these were unsavoury characters, one had not long come out of prison after shooting two coppers and another had been done for ABH, the things these people had done didn't bare thinking about, and all I could think about was my kids. I had three-year-old twin girls at the time, these weren't the sort of people that we needed around us. I think Mick was taken along with it all a bit, he wasn't really corruptible and could certainly stand his own ground that was for sure, but these were bad influences.

From time to time they'd often bugger off to different places, but it was usually either Blackpool or Sheffield, they had friends in both those places. Often, they'd go to Blackpool to sell little gimmicks and make a quid or two. Paul had a good friend in Blackpool and they all used to meet up there. I never went myself so I couldn't say for sure what they got up to, I wasn't interested, but I did overhear some tales and what I heard just made me want to know less, I'd heard people had been hurt and I was just a normal person, so it did open my eyes to what went off in other worlds, it made me very cautious knowing about that side of life.

This is how the main incident that blighted my life came about. We used to go most Saturday nights to Heppy's night spot in Wakefield. One night Paul and his then girlfriend Elaine came back to our house for some supper. They'd been at each other's throats all night prior to this, she wanted to be a gangster's moll and I got the impression that she just wanted to run with the bad boys. Paul, again with no boundaries was on the verge of battering her, so Michael stood up and got hold of Paul, Paul was pushing him away, but Michael got him in a hold that he couldn't get out of and I saw in Paul's eyes he was frightened. Being a wrestler back in the day Michael knew how to restrain people and he had the strength to back it up. Paul couldn't get away. He did the only thing he could do and bit into Michael's ear, it came away, it was horrific. Michael let go and swiped Paul with an uppercut, Paul ran for the hills. Michael had a Crossbow in the cellar, he went straight for it and ran out into the street, Sykesy was in a bit of a state from the main blow and had hidden under a van just down the road, so Michael came back to the house and I knew he needed to go to Hospital. So, another guy called Mick McGinley (the DJ from Heppy's at the time) who also used to come back to ours for supper, ran Michael to the hospital. The ear was quite bad, they grafted it back on, but it didn't take, and began to get infected, it had also damaged some of the internals of Michael's ear. Michael was kept in overnight, so Mick McGinley brought me back home and that's when it began to sink in. I sat on the sofa for half an hour, the shock of the situation, my head was spinning with the evenings events, when moments later someone barged through the door, I knew the face, but not the name, he said if you ring the police there will be problems, but it was too late, Michael had been to hospital and the police were already involved, even if we'd said nothing they knew who was involved. That was the beginning of some dark times.

The real problems came for the shop initially, I was running it while Michael worked, we'd built up a real nice business, but people knew of Paul and that he frequented there and people just stopped coming in. Even though he wasn't supposed to be around us Paul would come into the shop, just sit in the corner and say things to everybody and anybody, the most horrible things. Everyone on Lupest knew who he was, because at some point or other he'd caused everyone a problem. Then day by day custom began to drop off, no one wanted to be in the shop when Paul was around. He'd even invite his undesirables over to have discussions in the shop, people from all over the major cities, I used to say if the coppers knew that all these faces were here at the same time they'd cordon bloody Lupset off. Sheffield, Blackpool, Liverpool, and Barnsley to name but a few, these were real criminals. This, I think was Paul's way of letting me know that if I didn't retract my statement to the police I'd end up penniless.

Before encountering all this, I was brought up quite quietly, an only child, this world was something new to me and not something I wanted to be part of and definitely not something I wanted my kids to be near.

Eventually, we moved out of the shop, it was a council rented shop, but our own business, we just wanted to get away and that was because of Paul, his presence and the negativity towards our customers and staff meant the shop slowly died. I couldn't even get staff who were willing to work in there, one lady had lived on the Lupset estate all her life and she didn't stick around, and I wasn't willing to put other people's lives at jeopardy either, so it had to close.

In another incident, one which the twins were too young to really recall, was when he'd been told he wasn't to come anywhere near Michael, myself or any of the family. There was a snicket at the back of the shop and he used to come down there and he'd approached the twins and said, "Do you want to go to the seaside for the day", in today's terms he basically abducted them, they were kids and obviously they'd love to go to the seaside with Uncle Paul! He took them to the seaside, not for long but it was completely without our knowledge and permission, what could possibly have been going through that man's brain it was basically Kidnap.! They came back and said they'd had a lovely time, but I didn't say a word, Paul turned around and said, "What's wrong have you fallen out with me?" how his mind worked I will never know. After everything that had happened regarding the ear incident and the threats in his crazy mind he still thought everything could be fine, he was beyond deluded. On top of all that I knew he'd never had a driving licence in his entire life and he used to drive around like a looney tune anyway, the road was his and no one else's.

As these incidents continued, I began to think that if I went to the police, was he going to do anything to my children and my children were my life, even now, most likely he wouldn't have, but that was the nature of the unhinged man that loomed over our lives, and life was bad. When it came to the trial for the ear incident I was the main witness, but I received a call at home, and this rough voice said, "We know where your kids go to school, you get up on that stand you won't see your kids again". That was it for me, I couldn't risk anything happening to my children, I retracted my statement. I would do anything for my kids.

We then went to live at Walker Avenue. Paul still frequented there even though the shop had closed, his venue then became our house. In the run, up to the fight with John L Gardner, I can categorically tell you Paul didn't do any real training, he came to our house most days, completely unwelcome, this was the point I had become really fed-up of his presence, but he just wouldn't go away, I was genuinely scared. He sat with his back against our radiator drinking Whiskey that was his training! That is the honest truth and besides all that he shouldn't even have been in our house because of the police/court restrictions that had been placed on him for the ear incident, but that shows you how he just didn't care about any consequences that may come his way.

I went to a few of Paul's fights, but Michael went to them all. One of the ones I remember going to was when he fought Neil Malpass from Doncaster, the blood, the gore, the spit that went on at those fights, what for? That's just the wildness that followed Paul, it wasn't for me, I think Mick probably went to them all but not me.

We eventually moved to a house in Streethouse that we were doing up and months went by where we never saw or heard from Paul. Things began to pick up with Michael's building business, we had a row of houses, did them up and we went to live in Bridlington in a big white house that looked like a German castle, it had 6 bedrooms, I lived on the top floor. Things were looking up, we owned a block of flats, Hotel, big house and a bed and breakfast. Life was rosy for a time, but he wasn't gone yet.

Sometimes we'd go for a drink to a local pub (I was always the designated driver) Michael liked a real drink; the pub was in the old town across the road from the cop shop, one of our regulars. We walked in and who was sat there with that hang-on/idiot and ambassador of the Paul Sykes Fan Club but Mick Senior a notorious bull-shitter from our area, one of the Paul Sykes lovers who'd crowd around and listen to his crazy stories in awe.

Paul said, "I can see you're not pleased to see me" he'd got Mick Senior to track us down by asking around and he'd brought him across to find us. He said, "I'm stopping at yours tonight" by this time I'd grown a pair, got myself a suit of armour, he'd changed me, my personality even, I was often off with people, I had never been like that before. Anyway, I clearly let him know he wouldn't be stopping at ours. In some respects, he did me a favour he made me stronger, I progressed in my career and I was a much harder and more determined person, if I could get through what he'd done to me and my family, I could get through anything!

Anyway, he had absconded from a half-way house, his stop point before reintegrating into society, but again he'd defied the rules and made his way over to Bridlington with Mick Senior. Why would someone assist that, even for Paul's own good, but Mick Senior would do anything, the same man you see picking Paul up on release from Hull prison on the documentary Paul Sykes at Large.

Paul proceeded to tell us the tale of what he'd done, the details of which I can't remember but the crux was he said he needed to get out of the country and he needed us to help him, here was an opportunity I couldn't miss, I was petrified of Paul and his erratic behaviour, but to get him out of the country for good, I had to be in on that.

He said "I want you to lend me £600 and also nip into town and get me some socks, shorts, t-shirts, trainers etc. I'm going to Singapore". I jumped at the chance. "One other thing though" he said, "I need you to take me down there", meaning to the airport I presumed. I had a new car at the time, a Nissan Prairie people carrier type car, they'd just come out, it wasn't ideal. Michael couldn't drive after being in the pub, but I said to him, "I have to do this", I quickly nipped around town and got the things Paul needed for his trip, along with the money he'd asked for. I was doing it not just for me, but for everyone else, not even just my family, he hurt so many people in so many different ways, I was doing what had to be done. It was the worst journey of my life, by this point I didn't know if he would be fine and be grateful for the assistance or kill me, you just never knew with Paul he was capable of anything at any time. One minute he could be laughing telling jokes and the next second he could erupt. If I came back from this journey in one piece I would be happy, it was the scariest few hours of my life, just me and Paul in the car, but I was stronger now, I could do it. He directed us to a very specific travel agent in London's Piccadilly Circus, at this time he was well known to the authorities so he sent me inside to pick up the tickets, not willing to risk someone being there waiting to pick him up, so I did it, luckily without any problems. The tickets were pre-ordered.

He said, "Right let's have a bit of something to eat", which, of course meant that I was to buy him something to eat, "And then I need you to take me to Leicester", I bet my family were wondering where the hell I was. Even I didn't know, but somewhere in Leicester on the way back we had to call at someone's house, I don't know who, but Paul got out of the car went straight in and all I heard was blue murder and chaos, but I can only guess it was over money for his trip. Paul ran out and we drove up to Leicester Forest Services on the M1, Paul made me go up the trade/police only road. Even now, so close to the finish line he just didn't care, we could have easily been pulled by the police and he was instantly recognisable to the police forces in most areas.

He got out of the car, shut the door, and then he opened it again and he said, "Be careful driving home won't you Janet" what did that mean? It sent a shiver down my spine, but I just said, "Good Luck" not wanting any kind of scene, he actually gave me a tenner for the petrol to get back home, clearly that tenner came from my own money, but I had to appear grateful. Anyway, I headed straight back home as fast as I could, I put petrol in at the first opportunity, went to the toilet and I rang the pub and told Michael I was ok and where it was that I'd left Paul, none of it made any sense. I drove straight to the pub, and as soon as I got there I broke down, it had taken its toll on me, I didn't even know if I was coming back, Paul's brain had a thousand and one compartments with a different evil thought in each one, I was just glad to be home with my kids, it was over, again, or so I thought.

Sadly, that wasn't the end though. We got back on with life for a few weeks, I was elated, things were looking up again, I felt like I had been re-born, I kid you not. Then one morning I got a phone call, the voice at the other end of the phone said, "Mrs Sellers?" I said "Yeah" he said "Do you know an individual by the name of Paul Sykes?" and I said "Yeah" the wind was well and truly knocked out of my sails. I instantly felt like I'd dropped from 5'6" to 4'2". He then proceeded to tell me who he was, Douglas somebody from the British Embassy in Singapore He said, "Paul said if I rang this number you could wire him some money because, he's got no money and he's getting himself into a lot of trouble over here" so I said, "Well I'll see what I can do" and this Douglas guy gave me a contact phone number, along with this that and the other. I left it there hoping I would hear no more and they'd try someone else. Anyway, I had three phone calls in total in the same week so by the third time, I eventually said "Look, do you know who you're dealing with over there?" he said "Who?" I said, "Look if I were you I'd call the Home Office and ask them about Paul Sykes, because nobody is going to send any money over, but you'll get him over for free if you contact them, trust me". I got another phone call half an hour later saying, "Thank you Mrs Sellers". It was done. So, I was the one who got shut of him, but I was also the one who brought him back into the country, bitter sweet. I assumed Paul was back in the nick from that point and heard little else on the matter. We ended up moving back over Wakefield way to live in Normanton.

Sometime later I was working in TV/Media and I had been working on Last of The Summer Wine and I'd had to nip somewhere and was driving past Snapethorpe School, I was going along the road, and I saw this figure and I thought I know that person there, I slowed down and it was Sykesy and he was absolutely pissed out of his head he was, so I rolled the window down and shouted "Ya drunk bastard, where ye going?" and he goes "Who are you?" and I said "Don't you know me?" I saw the cogs turn and his face click at which he was just about to come across the road and I floored it out of there. Around that time, I'd heard tales that he was now on the down and out and that he was regularly being beaten up by local kids and drunken revellers themselves, but I never felt sorry for him, because that's what he'd spent his life doing to everybody else. What goes around comes around, Karma!

Life was good again. We'd moved back over this way to an old Pit House across from the Village Pub in Normanton, I'd set-up a business on the markets and I'd been across to Penistone, the weather wasn't too good so I was back early. Anyway, Michael walked in through the door and said, "I've got surprise for ya", it was Paul! He said to me "Well of all the people in the world that I know, I have never known anybody with balls as big as yours" I said, "What are ya talking about?" He said "It wa' you weren't it? you that snitched to the Police" and I turned around and said, "I've never snitched on anyone in my life, but you Paul, you've given us so much bloody grief and heartache that I wanted revenge" and he said, "There's nowt like revenge gone cold is there lass?" and he shook my hand. He thought I was a stupid housewife, but he'd underestimated me, I wasn't as daft as he thought.

I also knew his sister as well, she was a really nice girl, if there was anyone that Paul genuinely loved it was her, no one else, but he loved her. I knew Cath too, a really pretty girl, the cutest little girl you've ever seen, as well as Wendy another lovely girl. Why these people fell for him and his rough charm, bad boy reputation, I will never know, he always liked his girls bang on 16, probably more impressionable in their ways, mouldable to Paul, I can only think their lives will have also been vastly impacted by Paul's ways, just like mine was.

A lot of people think Paul was an intelligent man, my theory is he did that much time he'd passed so many exams and read so many books, he'd had the time to learn. Everyone knew Paul, up and down the country, for one reason or another, every police force, every prison, every city crook. There wasn't a right and wrong, there was only what Paul said, an undeniable Psychopath. In terms of the things he'd done to people and the time he spent in jail, it was nothing, in some ways even though he spent years in prison he got away with so much.

He loved kids, he wanted dozens of his own, but that doesn't make the things he'd done justifiable or make him a great person, but he was good with the kids generally.

Paul was Satanic from the word go, he probably had a pointed tail and horns, I honestly think we was born pure evil, whether that's right I'm not sure, but it is what I believe. Even now I won't even say "God rest his soul", cos he certainly hasn't gone up there. I do believe there is pure evil in the world and he was one of those.

# JOHN PURVIS

John Purvis is 59 and is from Wakefield's Lupset Estate and had been in prison with Paul a couple of times.

*       *       *       *

I heard the name Paul Sykes for the first time when I was in Armley Jail. I must have been only 17 or 18 and my cell mate at the time was a fella from a big well-known family in Bradford called Trotter. When this lad found out I was from Wakefield he said to me "you must know Paul Sykes then?" well I didn't know Paul Sykes and I hadn't heard of him before but this guy Trotter was in awe of Sykes and he went on to tell me how good mates they had been in Walton nick in Liverpool and how he used to train with this 'main man' of all the prisons. I couldn't help but get the impression that his fella Trotter idolised this Paul Sykes a bit.

I wouldn't get to meet Paul Sykes until around 1978 on the Eastmoor Estate. The first time I would see him would be in Norman Cunliffe's second hand shop and it was an extremely uncomfortable moment for the lad I was with Lance Jackson. Lance was the same age as me, about twenty at the time, and he had said something to Paul's girlfriend at the time, Wendy Doggett because Lance had been dating her for quite some time until she finished with him to go out with Paul. Wendy had told Paul and Paul was going to give Lance a right good hiding. So, Lance and I walked into the second-hand shop and there stood Paul Sykes. Luckily, at that time Paul only knew the name Lance Armstrong he didn't know what Lance looked like. So, as soon as Lance saw Paul he froze, Paul looked at him and then just carried on talking to Norman Cunliffe. Lance realised that Paul hadn't cottoned on that it was him and we got out of there as fast as we could. Lance couldn't believe how lucky he had been and I'm sure to this day he will remember that incident.

This will have been around the time that Paul turned professional as a Boxer and he was in the prime of his life. Lance really dodged a bullet that day I can tell you that because Sykesy would have murdered him if he had realised it was Lance. Lance told me afterwards he likened it to being caught in enemy territory and all he could think about was to act normal.

When I started going out drinking as an 18-year-old I used to see Paul about town, I'd usually see him in Heppy's most weekends and one of the nights I was in there I recall Paul knocking a bouncer out cold. As soon as he had connected with this guy's face he walked out of the place very cool and calm like something out of a John Wayne movie.

It must have been around the 1980's when I was to get really close up to Paul as I was doing a five-year sentence. I was in Hull Prison when it used to be a long-term Dispersal Unit. At the time Paul was only doing two and a half years but all the inmates doing over five years got as much gym time as they wanted, but because Paul was only doing thirty months he was hardly getting to go to the gym at all and he wasn't at all happy, which is putting it mildly. The screws were telling him that he was only a 'short termer' so he wasn't as entitled to the gym as the long termers to which Paul replied, "I've been a fucking long termer all my life".

One particular day, a gym screw called John Raine said to Paul "listen mate it's my fucking gym and I'll tell you when you can come to the gym" you can imagine can't you that Paul didn't take kindly to being told that at all and so whacked the screw breaking his jaw, he then turned on another screw and body punched him breaking his ribs. Although I wasn't there to see it I was a cleaner on C Wing and a couple of guys who were there told me what went on and then the sirens of two ambulances could be heard and it didn't take long to get around the prison grapevine that Sykesy had done in two screws. For his troubles Paul was handed another three and a half years to add to his two and a half year sentence, taking him to a grand total of six years thus entitling him to as much gym time as he wanted!

Hull wouldn't be the only Prison where I would encounter Paul as I also spent time with him when he was in Frankland Prison in County Durham.

One afternoon I was on a visit and I could see Paul Sykes across a table with Mick and Janet Sellers. I was having a visit with a guy called John who was also from Wakefield. After Paul had finished with his visit he came over and said to me, "are you from Wakefield?" He'd obviously seen John, who'd been up to visit me and he must have known him, "does he come and visit you often?" Paul asked, "has he bunged you owt" was his next question. These days in prison it's all drugs now but in them days if you got bunged anything it was usually a bit of cannabis or £20. John had given me a £20 note but I told Paul I hadn't been bunged anything because I knew that the likelihood was that he would have been after it. He asked where I worked and at that time I was working in the kitchen so I told him, "ah in the kitchens are ya, I'll be seeing ya later then" he said. So, a couple of days later I saw Paul in the exercise yard and he asked if I could get him a bit of meat out of the kitchen. I had to tell him no as I only had a week left to do and I didn't want to get nicked and end up having days added onto my sentence. As soon as I'd said no his whole face and demeanour changed and he shouted "ya fucking cunt I'll break ya fucking ribs ya bastard" I just walked off with a screw and left him ranting furiously away to himself. When I was in Frankland with him there wasn't one man in there, inmate or screw, who would front up to Sykesy, he was the top man in that Prison and I don't give a shit what any else says I've seen it with my own eyes, what Paul Sykes said more or less went! I've never come across anyone like him in prison and I doubt there will by anyone like him again. He got his own way with everything that he wanted to.

Paul's best friend in prison was Delroy Showers from Toxteth in Liverpool. Delroy was on my wing in Hull at the same time I was in there with Paul. Delroy was serving nine years for masterminding a cannabis deal. I'm sure Delroy was shipped to Frankland from Hull just to keep Paul quiet, he was a voice of reason with Paul. Paul was also good friends with Frankie Fraser's son David in Frankland. Paul had friends in the nick but none of them were as close to him as his friendship was with Delroy Showers, they would always be together in

Frankland.

Delroy was very powerfully built and could look after himself but he wasn't in the same league that Paul was for using his fists. Delroy's brother Michael was much more feared as a fighter and his name was well respected in prison. I think Delroy was that intelligent that he could get the things he wanted with words rather than with violence but he still wasn't someone to be messed with.

When Paul was living his second life as a tramp I would see him as I used to work the markets. Sometimes I'd go on a morning and he'd be laid asleep on cardboard boxes and he'd get up just like he was getting up out of bed, he'd have a stretch and stagger off looking for his morning drink. He looked like nothing then, he couldn't fight or defend himself either really. I dare say he could have been blown over by a gust of wind.

Paul Sykes at thirty, no one would have had a chance, no one I've ever met either on the out or in prison would have come close to beating Paul Sykes at thirty in his prime years. The people who used to walk past and kick him while he slept, or set his hair and beard on fire wouldn't have even dared to think of doing such a thing even just a few years before that. I saw him in his prime and I saw him towards the end of his life and it was like looking at a totally different man.

I have been in many prisons throughout my life and I must have been told fifty times at least "ah you're from Wakefield you must have heard of Paul Sykes, well my mate chinned him", what a load of bollocks! He was the real deal.

# TOM KIELY

Tom Kiely was a young top 10 Heavyweight who Paul took on in what was only his 3rd pro outing. Paul went on to beat Kiely on pts in a relatively close bout.

My research on Kiely led me to believe that he was a greatly avoided fighter at the time in the British Heavyweight Division and according to ex promoter John Spensley "he'd have made Mohammed Ali look bad as he was a Southpaw and was always standing on your feet". So, as much as it was a massive step for Paul Sykes taking on Kiely it was worth the risk as if he was successful it would catapult him into the British Top 10. It was a huge risk and from the reports I've read it was stalemate but Paul came out triumphant.

I tracked Tommy down via the Brighton Ex Boxers page on Facebook and he gave me his thoughts on his bout with Paul back in April 1978 at the Norfolk Gardens Hotel in Bradford.

\*     \*     \*     \*

I had heard of Paul Sykes in Jan/Feb of 1978, I remember it being a few months before I fought him anyway. Some of the London mob (Alex Steen) had gotten a hold of him and they were all raving on about him. The only thing I knew about Paul before we fought was that the guy had done a lot of porridge. Actually, I only had about a weeks' notice of the fight before I fought Paul and I didn't meet him until the weigh in on the morning of the fight. He was charging around like a lunatic trying to intimidate me but I wasn't interested in getting involved in his games.

Red Rum's jockey was the guest at the evenings boxing and I travelled up with the journalist/pundit Reg Gutteridge in the car for the fight.

I know I lost on points on the night but I felt like I was the clear winner. The fight I had against Sykes wasn't a very hard fight at all for me, at the time I was ranked 4th in the division. Even though it was only Paul's third fight all the talk at the time was about Paul Sykes v John L Gardner and everyone desperately wanted Paul to face John L. Gardner's team wouldn't let him fight me because they knew he'd have been an easy fight for me. Gardner just came forward all the time and didn't know anything else.

It's quite sad talking about it now as I was well and truly shunted out of the picture but what could I do when Micky Duff wouldn't let me near John L, but there you go, that's life.

To look at Paul Sykes it was obvious that he was a big, strong lump of a man, Sykes would have been great these days competing in that MMA cage fighting malarkey. I could tell when I was boxing him that he wasn't a mug but he found me hard to hit as I was very unorthodox in my style.

I wanted the opportunity to speak to Paul after our fight but I couldn't get to him due to him being surrounded with gangsters, then he left quite sharpish to go drinking.

As a boxer, I must be honest and say that Paul had no real skill, his game was always to over awe you with his freakishly raw physical strength. He had guts and determination in abundance as a fighter I have to give him that and he was fearless and as hard as a rock, but I still maintain that he was bloody lucky against me not that it matters now of course.

*"Boxing has always been in my blood, I was born to reach British Heavyweight Boxing level"*

**-P Sykes**

# COLIN HART

For me, Colin Hart is the No.1 Boxing writer in Britain by a landslide. He currently writes a fortnightly boxing column for The Sun Newspaper.

Colin was born in West Ham, London in 1935 and he's been a boxing writer since 1958 and has seen them all come and go in the fight game of British Boxing.

Colin is widely renowned as the "voice of boxing" certainly in Britain and he was also inducted into the International Boxing Hall of Fame in Canastota New York.

Colin spared me a little time to ask him a few questions on Paul Sykes and to tell me what he knew of Paul Sykes when he started his boxing career.

\*       \*       \*       \*

I covered Paul Sykes' fight with John L Gardner at Wembley Arena in June 1979. The big tough daddy of a dozen prison yards completely swallowed it when he came up to face Gardner.

Sykes was an incredibly feared man in the prison system, he was the No.1 in every prison he ever went into but when he climbed into the ring with John L it was a different story, John L boxed his bloody ears off and he cowered away in round Six.

Paul Sykes was notorious and had spent around Thirteen years inside before he turned over to the pro ranks. Paul, relatively quickly, forced his way in to being a title contender.

Outside of the ring everyone was terrified of him and he was a real hard nut. I'd heard a lot of tales of Sykes fighting in clubs and beating people up very badly on a weekly basis.

The night when Paul fought Gardner you had this man who could beat anyone on the cobbles and Paul was so much bigger then John L, well by about 4 inches and god knows how many inches in reach but he didn't use it to his advantage in a boxing sense.

I'll never forget the moment Paul Sykes spewed it and turned his back on Gardner, he was a complete coward. Any respect Paul Sykes had gained in the boxing world or with the press evaporated in the few seconds it took him to turn his back.

It doesn't surprise me in the slightest that Sykes only fought once after that and that it was in Africa. Sykes was ridiculed after the Gardner fight for sure.

From a boxing writers point of view, when Paul Sykes lost his title fight nobody bothered with him again.

Sykes had a very sad ending to his life but I can see why people see him as an interesting story to read about. As a boxing writer Paul Sykes was brought to my attention from a work point of view but truthfully, I was never a fan of the man.

# LANCE JACKSON

Lance Jackson is 59 years old and is from the Lupset Estate. Lance now resides in Dudley in the West Midlands but he told me with great pride that he's a 'Wakey lad'.

I initially heard about Lance Jackson from the interview that John Purvis had given me and through the wonders of social media I managed to track Lance down.

Lance told me that even though he had had a few awkward moments with Paul he'd always found him to be incredibly fascinating to observe in close quarters, he likened it to a camera man filming the wildlife, risking life and limb to get award winning shots.

*       *       *       *

If you grew up where I did you heard the name Paul Sykes a lot. I was 12 years younger than Paul Sykes but the group of people I knocked about with knew who this local legend was, in terms of his exploits, and the fact that he was a boxer.

To be honest I think people underestimated his capabilities as an athlete because he was a tremendous natural athlete. Paul had all the physical attributes to get to where he was when he was in his heyday. He had a perfect body that enabled him to recover quickly from training. Paul had so much going for him physically but of course he spent the prime of his life between the ages of 17 to 30 in the nick!

Everything I heard about Paul Sykes before I met him was violence related. It was well known Paul had been a good amateur boxer and he showed a lot of promise up to about the age of 17 years old which was when he first went away.

The first time I met Paul was quite a nervous time to say the least. He'd nicked my girlfriend, the bastard ha ha! I had been seeing Wendy Doggett for around six to seven months. She liked a name did Wendy, she liked somebody who had a little bit of a reputation and so when Paul Sykes got out of the nick I suppose he had the ultimate name in her circle.

Wendy was also best friends with a girl called Cath Wilby and they had been in the same class at school. Paul was with Cath first, I think she was pregnant at the time, but I'm sure he was with Wendy too at this point. Paul gravitated towards my girlfriend Wendy and they took up together but I think Paul was torn between both girls. Cath was small and pretty whereas Wendy was really glamorous looking and had the height of a model being almost six feet. The inevitable happened and Wendy eventually dumped me and like I said she took up with Paul and although I was really pissed off and heartbroken I quickly realised there was not a great deal I could do about it. When she left me for Paul, I don't know why but, the word around Lupset was that Paul Sykes was gonna give Lance Jackson a good kicking.

So, one day I saw Paul Sykes in a shop on the Eastmoor estate, Paul was stood there and he really was quite a distinguished figure when I first clapped eyes on him. I was with John Purvis and a few others at the time and I told them that I had heard that Paul was going to give me a hiding but that I was going to go in and front it out with him. John said I was mad and I might as well commit suicide but I told him it was my decision and I just wanted to get it over with. Call me crazy but I went into the shop and I introduced myself to Paul, "Hello Paul I'm Lance Jackson I hear you're looking for me", Paul was completely taken aback by this and maybe he even admired my bravery/stupidity because he just smirked and said, "Nah I haven't got any problems with you lad". I went to shake his hand, well I'm quite a bit bloke at six feet six inches tall and as I went to shake his hand he told me to be gentle and not to squeeze it as he had really injured it. This was only a couple of days after his first professional bout with Keith Johnson. I don't know, maybe if I had caught him on another day then he might have been different but he wasn't nasty and we had a chat. It was sort of just laughed off that he had nicked my girlfriend.

Looking back, being nearly 60 now it was rather foolish of me to confront Sykesy like that but I was only around 19 at the time and I must have had a peanut for a brain. One thing I do remember saying to Paul was asking him about his boxing as I'd always been a huge fan of the fight game. Paul said something to me along the lines of "When you're in prison your life is on hold, I haven't aged past 21 because I've been locked up away from temptations and bad habits". I wished Paul good luck in his career and I told him I'd follow him with great interest. I was also relieved that I wasn't due a kicking anymore!

I'd always been aware of Paul around town and when I would see him I would always have this terrible sense that he was a very lonely man. He didn't have friends he had people who hung around him like ants to jam as if his fearsome reputation was going to rub off on them because everyone feared Paul Sykes.

Paul was a very dangerous and volatile individual and the next story I tell you will give you some more insight into that. Paul could change from being very friendly to someone to beating the living daylights out of them for the slightest thing.

One night, about 18 months after I had smoothed everything over with Paul, I had come home on leave (I was in the army at the time) and it was the middle of the week and like most places midweek a Tuesday and Wednesday night are nowt nights aren't they. So, I called into The Strafford Arms and who did I see in there but Paul Sykes. There was hardly anyone else in at the time, Paul saw me and shouted me over to join him for the night and we started chatting away. To be honest I wasn't exactly comfortable in his company because we weren't really mates so to speak, we only had the one common denominator and that was a bit of a sore point with me at the time. I don't know how it happened but I ended up going out with him for the full night and it was a very interesting exercise to say the least.

Everywhere we went the licensee would know him, they always

greeted him by name and he rarely paid for anything. I remember going into The Wine Lodge (now Montgomery's) and Paul went up to the bar and ordered about six drinks and he just didn't pay for them, the bar staff didn't look surprised at all. It was a unique experience for me and that was the pattern that followed all evening. Even at the end of the night when we went to a café on Cheapside called 'Parthenon' Paul just started grabbing handfuls of sausages and eating them in front of the owners, the owner was helpless and stood smiling saying, "Hello Paul" I felt for the owner it made me feel sick to be honest. It was like walking around with a big bully.

We were sat in this Café when Paul said, "Do you want to come back to mine for a few drinks? It'll be nice for you to catch up with Wendy". So, being the fucking idiot that I was at the time and after six pints I thought it sounded like a good idea and we went back to his bachelor pad in Ossett. When I went in I could see Paul must have been doing really well in life financially speaking as his place was beautiful. Paul got me a drink and excused himself and left me and Wendy chatting. When Paul left the room, Wendy asked me "What you doing back here?" and she seemed very uneasy, panicking almost. Then Paul walks back in from the bedroom and he's in nothing but his underwear, as you can imagine my next thought was "What the fucks going on here?". "Don't mind me I like to be comfortable" he said. Then the conversation started to take a turn, he started to ask about me and Wendy and asking me awkward questions like "How many times do you think you fucked her?", at this point, even though I'd had a few drinks I was sobering up rapidly. Wendy was telling Paul to behave and I was hoping to be beamed up by Scotty but it wasn't happening and Paul's mood had really started to change for the worse and he was getting really aggressive verbally, even his body language was different. Paul left the room for a second time and as soon as he was out of earshot Wendy turned to me and said, "Get the hell out of here now Lance I've seen this before and it doesn't end well". I didn't need telling twice and I flew out of the door and didn't look back. I'd like to thank Wendy for that, she knew him better than most and the look on her face that night was of sheer panic, maybe she had some insight into what was about to happen and saved my life. She knew Paul and she knew what he was capable of.

During that night, out when we were in the pub Paul had put his hand on my chest saying that he thought I was a "Big fella", at the time I was a soldier and I was into power lifting so I was in good shape. I never knew it then, otherwise I wouldn't have even gone back to his house, but I've heard the stories of him in Jail, of him being involved in male rape and I just think and thank god that Wendy was there that night. From that evening on I made sure that I was never in a one on one situation with Paul Sykes again. I can never be sure of what would have happened that night, maybe nothing or maybe that good hiding had been waiting for me all along but I'm glad I never hung around to find out.

On that night out, Paul would talk about his philosophy on life. Paul would say that the reason he never paid for anything is that people had a healthy respect for him and so why should he pay. He said if people didn't show him respect he'd "Tab their lugs". When Paul wasn't talking about hurting people he spoke like a very intelligent man, he was extremely articulate as well, but the circle he moved in would never encourage that. There's no doubt that Paul Sykes under a different set of circumstances and in my humble opinion could have been not only a great athlete but a great man in general, he could research and retain knowledge very easily and he would regurgitate information at the drop of a hat. He was a smart guy and it's a shame that his life took the path that it did. He was someone who could have really left his mark in a positive way and he could have contributed a lot to society. When you read Sweet Agony, you can tell that it wasn't written by some halfwit, his brain was naturally intelligent and he was very well read.

Many years later I came out of the army and I was running a security company with Gavin Hepworth (who was in Unfinished Agony) called Master Guard. We used to do a variety of things from training dogs to doing the doors. There was a rival company but it was a friendly rivalry and it was run by a guy called Les Carr. Basically, what happened was that everyone in Wakefield who owned a pub got together for their own protection and Les Carr was on a retainer. The agreement was that if Sykesy went into any of those pubs they could call Les Carr and he would turn up and turf Paul out because he was the only man in Wakefield who could physically match Sykesy and go toe to toe with him. Les Carr was 6ft 6inches, a 6th Dan Karate expert and had been on the England Karate team.

Over the years I would see Paul Sykes and his deterioration from being this magnificent athlete that he was in his early 30's to being fucked by the time he reached his mid 40's. A lot of times I would see him at ten in the morning and he would already be pissed.

One morning I was going up town and I saw two police officers arresting him for breaking his ASBO. He'd been barred from the centre of the city but kept coming back and therefore getting himself locked up. Paul became quite self-pitying and always had a whiney attitude with the police wanting to know why they were always picking on him. The morning I saw him getting arrested he was moaning like a little boy. Once over it would have taken ten officers to take Paul in and he wouldn't have been moaning he would have been throwing punches.

There were many people, towards the end of Paul's life that took the opportunity to give him a good kicking. The ironic thing is that the people who did give him a good hiding weren't his contemporaries that he'd wronged but they were the younger kids who were looking to build a reputation because Paul had become an easy target.

Things had become really bad for Paul towards the end of his life and I think this was one of the reasons Paul flung himself into the Wakefield Baptist Church, it was the church that took Paul in when he was poorly and it was shortly after this time that he died.

Paul was a shambling, drooling wreck at the end of his life and it wasn't pretty I'm afraid.

I would often see Walter Sykes around Lupset. It was well known that father and son had an extremely uneasy relationship to say the least. Paul spent his adult life giving his dad what for at any available opportunity he could for the way he had been brought up by him. I'd heard him many times call Walter a useless bastard.

Mr. Sykes had a very domineering personality. He made Paul go boxing as a lad and Paul obviously resented that. Paul was brought up with far too much discipline than was necessary. Mrs. Sykes was a nice woman but Mr. Sykes was never liked on Lupset.

You can't ignore that Paul Sykes is part of Wakefield for good or for bad and a lot of people will only know of Wakefield because of Paul Sykes.

Paul Sykes was physically gifted, more so than any other human being I've ever met. He was massively flawed though with a huge chip on his shoulder and he thought this world owed him everything when it fact it owed him nothing.

If Paul had grown up in a loving supportive home and encouraged to develop than possibly things may have been very different for him, he had the tools to do great things but instead used them in a negative way most of his life. Ultimately, Paul self-destructed.

That night I went back to Paul and Wendy's that was a month before he fought the Nigerian guy, Ngozika Ekwelum in Lagos in March 1980. So, when I went on that night out he was 'in camp' and I remember saying to him "How does drinking fit in with your training?" his answer was "Nothing wrong with having a drink of beer it keeps me regular and it helps me sleep". I didn't tell him but I remember watching the amount of alcohol he drank that night and thinking "I don't think it does pal". When Paul did fight in Africa he got fucking hammered in one round. After I'd heard Paul lost I remember thinking "is it any wonder he got hammered if his pre-fight training camp was anything to go by?". This guy who Paul boxed had fought Mohammed Ali and John L Gardner and Paul didn't even train for it properly, absolutely crazy!

I dare say that you could start professional boxing at thirty, have his physical attributes and his intelligence and become a success providing that you obey the other rules of professional boxing which are to keep yourself in good nick but Paul was just winging it. He thought he didn't need to be in the gym everyday dedicating himself to his craft, he relied too much on his natural ability but hampered that by going out drinking all the time and it took its toll.

*"I would probably be dead from syphilis by now"*

**-P Sykes**

*When asked where he would be if he had beaten John L Gardner

# ALAN LORD

Back in 1990, Strangeways Prison was taken over by hundreds of prisoners, it was all over the news at the time and I'm sure many of you remember the scenes of the dozens of prison inmates that had taken to the rooftops. Two people lost their lives and there was over £60m worth of damage done.

At the time, the prisoners said that it wasn't so much the environment that they were protesting about but the alleged physical brutality by the Prison Officers together with the lack of proper toilet facilities and being locked in their cells twenty-three hours a day.

The protest which lasted a total of twenty-five days left the prison authorities a lot of questions to answer and as a direct result of this riot there were many radical changes made to the prison system and Strangeways was rebuilt at a cost of £90m and renamed HMP Manchester.

Alan Lord became a key figure during the riots and even negotiated with authorities during the siege. After he was captured by a snatch squad it signalled the beginning of the end of the rooftop drama. Alan had been jailed for 15 years as a teenager for murder after a botched robbery.

Alan is 55 years old now and after serving thirty-two years, after time added on for a string of escapes and a few bust ups inside, he is now a free man and has turned his life around. He now runs a gym in Radcliffe and puts his energy into this and warning youngsters about offending saying that "prison will never be a bed of roses".

I managed to get in touch with Alan with the help of my publisher

Warcry Press and I had a strong feeling that Alan, with his thirty-two years in prison, must have come across the 'daddy of a dozen exercise yards' Paul Sykes.

*      *      *      *

I went into prison as a youngster, only 19 years of age, I didn't know a great deal but Paul Sykes' name was banded around prisons the whole length of the country.

The first time I saw Paul, this man that I had heard so much about, was in Strangeways in 1981. He was passing through Strangeways on the 'Ghost Train'. I'd only just got there and Paul was doing a power lifting competition and on first impressions I thought he was a huge, powerful and imposing figure of a man, a ridiculously strapping fella up close. The main thing which struck me looking at him was his aura and just how animated he was. He was very outspoken that day, he was a man who spoke his mind there was no doubt about that.

After the power lifting competition, which of course Paul won, a Prison Officer wanted to present the trophies but Paul pushed his way to the front and told him in no uncertain terms that he would be presenting the trophies, no one else! I could tell people were taken aback by his brazen attitude but never the less he got his own way and presented the trophies that day.

He lifted weights all the time and I saw him get bigger with every day that passed. He was of course alcohol free and he was eating quite well so was looking every inch of the icon that he had become with other inmates.

I would see Paul passing through various prisons as the years went by and I was later to bump into him at the back end of the 1980's in Frankland Prison in the Dispersal Unit.

Wherever Paul went he carried this tag of being the most dangerous prisoner in England! Would I agree with that? Well yes and no. At the end of the day I've met many prisoners, not as imposing as Paul

Sykes was, but I've met inmates that were 10st dripping wet but they were still people that you didn't mess with because a lot of these people weren't ever going to get out of Jail, they had nothing to lose, they had no qualms about getting another life sentence on top of the one that they already had, they might not have had the iconic status that Paul Sykes had but places like Frankland Dispersal Unit were full of these dangerous fuckers. Those type of offenders aren't curious about who you are, if you're the best fighter in England or how much money you have, a lot of the time it just comes down to whether or not you can stick up for yourself. Some of those prisoners aren't capable of that but they'll think nothing of getting a knife and stabbing you to death over a box of matches!

There were many stories over the years that followed Paul from prison to prison. I didn't pay them much heed as I always liked to make my own mind up about people and we all have good and bad sides to us. You should try to ignore what other prisoners might tell you about a person until you've met them, got to know them and found out what they're about. The prison grapevine can be full of tall stories and many of these stories are started because someone wants to manipulate and undermine someone else.

I never saw Paul behave inappropriately or take liberties with anyone, I never saw him try to impose himself on anyone else because he was a boxer or because of his hard case reputation. I think even Paul knew, as hard as he was, that he could never be that naive to think he could push people about whilst he was in the Dispersal Unit. He was an extremely bright bloke he will have had his wits about him living amongst the prisoners that were in there. The Dispersal Unit is like being in a prison inside a prison, he was in the company of the worst of the worst in there.

I'll say one thing about Paul, people respected him not only because he could fight but because he could have been the British Heavyweight Champion, he was good.

The last time I was in Prison with Paul was in 1997 in Woodhill nick in Milton Keynes, by then Paul was 51 years old. Paul just wanted some peace and quiet and he struggled with all the noise that there was on a night. He would be cranky and going mad in the morning because of the lack of sleep, he'd be shouting at the screws and demanding to see the Governor. He would get in to see the Governor and run his mouth off screaming that he should have control of his prison then he'd get placed on report and sent down to the block. He really did struggle in those later years, prison was just too busy for him.

I didn't listen to the rumours I'd heard about Paul, I got to know him and took him at face value, I think more people should have done the same.

# CLYDE BROUGHTON

Clyde Broughton was born in Hillsborough, Sheffield on the 12th August 1960, the son of the local Coal Man. He began to get into trouble from an early age, quickly progressing from Borstal to serious Prison time for a spate of robberies.

Now living in Wybourn, Sheffield he was already known to our publisher for his connections with Paul Sykes through the interviews they had done with him for his own book, which is currently still in the making and provisionally titled 'Gaol Hawk' it should hopefully be out sometime soon and has a Facebook page of its own if you want to keep up to date with its progress. Clyde wanted to keep a lot of his stories under wraps for obvious reasons, including those about his friendship with Paul Sykes, but he was happy to give us some insight into Paul Sykes for this book.

*　　*　　*　　*

My good friend 'Sykesy', What more can I say that hasn't already been said? A legend of a British Heavyweight and man, many stories, many rumours, and many of them in my opinion simply ammo to ruin the reputation and memory of a man they really couldn't control.

Paul was a friend of mine from the moment I met him, both in and out of the big house, sometimes bizarre, and sometimes out of order, but always loyal as far as I was concerned.

A lot of the rumours I deem to be nothing more than second hand nonsense, if you didn't know Paul at the time then you never will know or understand the Paul they talk about today.

Contrary to what you'd think I didn't meet Paul in the nick. I first met Paul on the out in my local pub after he had come over to Sheffield with Davy Dunford. Never the less, most of the time I spent with him was further down the line, certainly in the nick and more so in the gym, where usually weight training was our only relief from the tedium of being banged up.

Anyway, the first time I saw Paul he'd come in to the Springwood Pub in Sheffield on the Manor, that's the Woodthorpe area, the place always had a pretty bad reputation, but it was still one I'd regularly frequent.

Paul came over with a couple of guys who are mentioned in his book 'Sweet Agony', by the name of Davy Dunford, a local villain, and another black guy in a Rolls Royce, who I knew to be Delroy Showers from Liverpool, who was another character I was to later meet in the nick. Delroy and his brother Michael were notorious in shall we say the Underworld, but a thoroughly nice guy all the same, in fact further down the line Delroy would nickname me 'Nephew'. Even this year when we hooked up again, the words out of his mouth were "how's it going Nephew" clearly, I couldn't be his nephew, you know what I'm saying, but that was his joke.

That day I was in the Springwood with my pals and I was only about 16 or 17 years old, and a fair bit younger than Paul and his associates. They'd come in, I believe, to put the frighteners on another local guy called Freddie Bonzo or 'Fat Fred' as we called him, anyway thankfully that day Bonzo never showed or I think all hell would have broken loose. Paul was a man-mountain, and clearly brought in as muscle, he made a point of taking Fred's usual spot at the bar. The day passed without event, I'd heard of Paul Sykes before, but that was the first time I'd really set eyes on him.

Sometime later, again before prison, I met Paul in the very same pub, this time I put myself forward, we struck up conversation and instantly became life-long friends. It involved him saying some cheeky things about my missus, but we were on the same level and it was never a problem.

At the time, we were also grafting in some of the same circles, I was from Sheffield and he was often working with the main players from our area, such as Davy Dunford and Davy Lee etc. so we were bound to meet up and as grafters do at some point that would be in prison, I knew that, but from that day forth we were firm friends.

He had such a great sense of humour and he was very, very clever, he'd always act daft, but when it came down to it he'd out talk you and he'd out fight you, how do you deal with that? They say there's a fine line between a genius and a mad man and Paul was both.

Years later, on the inside I was doing a seven stretch for three robberies, it was then that I met Paul on the inside in Armley Prison, Leeds. We spent a lot of time together in many jails, mostly in the North. Paul ruled the prison system, his cell was always open and he did what he pleased. Being his close friend, I often picked up the same privileges, most mornings I'd head over to his to cell to play Chess, if he was playing Chess with me he wasn't causing the screws any problems, so it made sense.

Again, pretty much whenever we felt like it we'd head down to the gym to do weights. I was already powerful, and for a spell I did very well at it setting a couple of records in the system. Sykesy saw how good I was at it and chose me to train with him whenever possible, even though I was smaller than Paul, I was stronger. Paul wasn't really built for weights, don't get me wrong he was strong, but he was a big lad with great long arms, like a fucking gorilla. Initially he was powerful but he just didn't know how to do it right, there are techniques involved and I brought him on even though I was a lot younger than him, but he never moaned he just got on with it. In return, we used to go on the bag and he'd show me how to throw some combos and the basics of Boxing.

In all honesty, I was more of a footballer, I loved football. In fact, I never knew but it came to light when I hooked back up in Leeds with Delroy and Jamie through this very book that Delroy had thought I was the best footballer he'd ever seen and had written a poem about my skills, I never knew until just this year. I can honestly say I enjoyed those times inside, they were great, not many would say that though I'm sure.

In the prison system, I got to see Paul's interactions with all manner of characters, whether screws or prisoners, he wound the lot up including the lifer Bronson. Let me tell you no one was more feared than Paul within the system, and none got their own way like he did.

I never actually went to any of Paul's professional fights for one reason or another, but I knew I was in his thoughts, he actually sent me an original still photograph, not one previously circulated of himself mid-clash with the American Fighter Dave Wilson, the fight that ultimately ended up in Wilson spending 28 days in hospital, it simply read on the back in Paul's own hand writing 'To Clyde, my mate and one of the strongest kids Yorkshire has produced. All the best forever, Paul Sykes'.

Anyway, I apologise for the depth of my contributions to this book, its merely a scratch on the times I had with Paul, but there are plenty more tales, some hilarious about my times with Paul, but I have to save them for my own book, which is not just about me and Paul but about my time served, the crimes that resulted in it and some of the notorious characters I met in the prison system such as Robert Maudsley the Cannibal Killer, Ramsay Shannon, Bronson and the Black Panther to name a few. I've done spade with them all. It's been a bumpy ride let me tell you but of them all Paul was probably the greatest friend I made along the way. Keep an eye out for 'Gaol Hawk' to be released by Warcry Press soon.

# MARK SELLERS

Son of Mick Sellers RIP

Mick Sellers was quite a big part of Paul's own book, Sweet Agony and as Mick Sellers has sadly passed away now I thought it would be great to hear from Mick's Son Mark about his side to the stories.

*　　　*　　　*　　　*

My Dad featured heavily in Paul Sykes' book Sweet Agony, most of what was written was centred around Dad's friendship with Paul and the subsequent falling out over the ear biting incident that happened at our house. 'Boxer bites off Wrestlers Ear' it read in the Daily Mirror, but to me that was my Dad and my Uncle Paul.

Paul and my Dad were friends right from primary school, they used to fight like brothers would do when they were young, just like me and my own brother did, but they always remained friends at the end of the day.

My Dad Mick was the size of four men, the only person who could put Sykes on his arse. He could lift car engines out with his bare hands, he was forever working on motors and was a great mechanic as well as a great builder, an area in which he made some real money further down the line.

In the early days, my Dad and Paul were always wheeling and dealing together, though more so Paul. He often used our yard, shop, and even house at times as a centre for crooked business deals.

Villains from out of the area would often turn up for discussions in our yard, from places like Blackpool, Sheffield and sometimes further afield, but mainly the crowd from our area consisted of My Dad (Big

Mick Sellers or Suggsy as he was often known), Paul Sykes, Paul Burke and John Lloyd.

Paul Sykes who acted as the muscle, John Lloyd (a local Carpenter), his dad, a man by the name of Fred Lloyd had a scrap yard near the Double Two Factory and as such was the ring leader and Paul Burke, the main man, the money man. Paul always somehow managed to muscle in and take over. A tribe of shall we say small time gangsters, crooks, petty thieves, swindlers, whatever you wanted to call them. I'm not being biased in saying my Dad was one of the nicer of the bunch, with a greater work ethic. Some of that bunch were simply greedy men who would do anything and everything to make a quick quid.

Paul Sykes and my Dad were genuinely best friends from about the age of 4 and I always called him 'Uncle Paul' I always thought of him as a generous man and very funny, he would always involve us in adult humour and I thought it was hilarious at that age, but looking back it was probably a little inappropriate.

It has since come to light, after discussions with my Mum, that maybe the situation wasn't as clear cut as that and that maybe somewhere down the line as a child I had not fully realised the nightmare he created for my parents and particularly more so my Mum. Some of the stories in Sweet Agony are clear fantasy e.g. about my mum being sweet on Paul, which really upset my older brother Stuart. If you read further on in my mum's interview for this same book you will realise that she despised Paul and was smitten on my old man. That said I can honestly say my personal opinion was just that he was a funny and generous man, based upon the dealings I'd had with him, those were my memories from childhood.

One incident I remember was when we'd left the shop and moved to Walker Avenue, a clear memory, my memory has been very good from birth, almost photographic. Even though Paul came around to ours all the time this one incident stands out. One Christmas Day morning, when I was only eleven, Paul turned up with his son Paul Jnr, my Mums parents were there also (My Grandma and Grandad). Now, I didn't understand what he was saying at that age but I remember the conversation clearly. My Grandad said to Paul Jnr, "Did you get anything nice for Christmas Paul?" and he said "Yeah, I got a blow-up doll with real pubic hairs ... but I licked em all off!" I remember thinking what on earth is he on about I was only eleven, but looking back I'm thinking who on earth says those kinds of things, especially in those days, in front of Grandparents and Children, you just didn't do it.

That Christmas my Grandad had also made the twins (my younger sisters) some wardrobes for their Barbie dolls and when Paul Jnr came into the room he stood on one and basically trashed it, my Granddad was a very quiet man, and not well at the time, he never said a word, but his face said it all that day. Not the way a family Christmas should be, I guess the apple never falls far from the tree.

My Dad himself was a wrestler in his younger days, he could really handle himself, forever knocking people out, when needed. He taught me a few moves that came in handy further down the line when I was working the doors in Pontefract and Wakefield etc. My father was nice guy, a little corrupt, but not of a temperament like Sykes. The circles they moved in and the pubs that they frequented in there was always trouble.

One time my Dad was in the pub on Heath Common and someone tried it on, they came at him with a house brick in a carrier back, not a smart move regardless, but what happened next you couldn't make up! With the very first swing the brick broke straight through the carrier bag and flew in the opposite direction across the room, the power my Dad had, well he hit the guy and he flew across the room like something from a cartoon. Paul and my Dad used to fight entire pubs.

An interesting thing that not a lot of people know about and the reason that Paul had wanted Wakefield Cathedral on the cover of Sweet Agony was that my Dad once bet Paul £20 he couldn't touch the cock on the spire. Paul did it and they both went and got pissed on the proceeds. It was scaffolded up, but was 75 metres high! But Paul still did it, you'd have to be genuinely insane to do that, I don't think it would have mattered if it was twenty pence or twenty quid, he'd have still had a go at doing it.

I always looked up to my Uncle Paul, I used to baby sit his kids for him back in the day for a tenner, which was a lot back then, he was a very generous man. I don't have a bad memory of Paul, but I learnt later on that he was not as honourable as I'd remembered.

Another story that involved Paul bubbling my Dad was that the lads had gone to Sheffield to a warehouse that had copper piping and gas fires in it, Dad hadn't gone along but Dad sold one of the gas fires to his Dad and had given Paul the money, and Grandad had the fire installed. Then suddenly at 3am in the morning someone went around to grandad's house, told him the tale and took it back. Mum then got a phone call from the police in Sheffield to say Dad was locked up, it turned out Paul Sykes had been collared and grassed Dad up, they let Paul out, but that just goes to prove that he had no regard for anyone, even his closest friends and fellow crooks.

A couple of other incidents I remember, but not in detail was when Paul once told my Dad he needed to borrow £500 to buy a property in Devon, which turned out to be completely made up.

Another time I heard they were all in the car together and drove past Wakefield Prison, two screws were leaving and Paul pulled out what may or may not have been a replica gun and pointed it at them, just for fun, imagine the repercussions. Just crazy little incidents like that to Paul were nothing, but for many others they would have been a big deal, that was the crazy life that he led.

Another character from Sweet Agony that Dad (and us, the family) and Paul associated with was Norman Heald known as 'Chick-Heald' in the criminal fraternity a gentlemen crook from a place near Wakefield but out towards Barnsley way. An honourable thief, if there is such a thing, he excelled at clearing out stately homes, he was a serious criminal but a generous man who would look after his friends whenever a big sting had come off.

Norman was a respected older criminal but he was always wary of Paul as well. He's passed on now, he died in prison after being fitted up by the police for 'going equipped' he was no angel but that day he had genuinely been going to do some work on his Son's house when he'd been pulled with crowbars, and hammers etc. In fact, it was Norm who introduced me to my current trade as a Locksmith, I can pick many of the most intricate of locks in seconds, it was a master thief who'd sent me down that track, unknowingly, I now do work with the police as a Locksmith.

My Dad, although he was involved in bits and bobs, had a great work ethic. When we were kids we were made to work, I'd be under wagons from a young age, I remember one story of my Dad working on a roof and he tied our Stuart to the Chimney stack with a piece of rope and had him cleaning out the gutters, picture that and imagine it happening today!

The guys he used to hang out with were small time gangsters and greedy men. They used to take us down to old Black Sammy's to deal in old motors. They'd often take Paul with them and my Dad would come back and say, "never paid for them parts" with a wink, basically because Paul was there. Paul though was on another level when it came to intimidation, not just a crook, petty thief or swindler, he was into everything, he would do anything, usually violence, even to the brink of death he didn't care. Aside from the Boxing he had many a bare-knuckle fight against local gypsy gangs, he was fearless as far as I knew.

Paul also taught my brother to box and used him as a sparring partner. I'm a big lad but my brother, our Stuart, or 'Monkey Arms' as we called him because his arms literally extended right down to his knees in a hanging position like an Orang-utan, well if he got you by the throat you couldn't do anything about it. Imagine that, the reach on him, if Paul could deal with that in the Boxing Ring, he could deal with most things. My Brother spends most of his time in the States now working, but he'd often spar Paul. Sykesy used to say to my brother Stuart that he'd be the next big Heavyweight Boxer, but he didn't see it through.

I remember for a short spell Uncle Paul appeared to have some money, I'd been to the old farm house type house in East Ardsley, it was done up nice, it had handcuffs positioned all around the fire place as decorations. He didn't really have money he would just take over places, he'd turn up, take over and then your problem was, how are you going to get him out?

My Dad and Paul would regularly visit Manchester picking up stock then on to Blackpool selling trinkets and pulling the wool over people's eyes. Paul was always having someone over, he once sold someone a very large men's ring with a Cubic Zirconia in place of a Diamond for a sizeable sum, sooner or later the purchaser of the ring found out it wasn't real and he came back not knowing anything about Sykes and took a real hiding just for asking for his money back.

Sadly, my father Michael died on a Thursday in 1991 after an incident in a pub in Normanton. Even right until the very end he was fighting, jumped by a young coward in the toilets of his local, the Village Pub in Normanton, another youngster trying to make a name for himself and the injuries sustained ultimately led to my father's death, the fighting had caught up with him in the end, god rest his soul.

*"I began boxing when I was 7 years old and by the time I was 16, I was 6ft 1' and NABC champion"*

**-P Sykes**

# ALAN BROWN

Alan Brown is from Tyneside and is 53 years old. Alan told me he wasn't the best behaved as a young lad and spent a fair few years in various prisons such as Durham, Frankland and Belmarsh to name a few, because of his silly youthful antics. Being in these prisons meant that there was a pretty good chance he was going to have come across the notorious Paul Sykes in at least one of these and it was to be in Durham Jail that Alan first met Paul. Here is what Alan went on to tell me.

*     *     *     *

The first time that I heard about Paul Sykes was when I went to Durham Jail in 1984, Paul wasn't in the prison at that point but I often heard rumours about him being the hardest man in the system and that he had a liking for young YP's although he was still respected even though this went against the prison code! He also had a reputation and was well respected as a fighter and there wasn't anyone that was more feared then Paul Sykes was in the 1980's.

I wouldn't bump into the man until 1986 when I was in Durham again serving a different sentence. I was working serving the inmates their food on D Wing and on this day, it was my job to dish out the chips. I was specifically told only one scoop of chips to each prisoner so one scoop it was until in front of me stood this man mountain, it was 'Sykesy' he held out his tray and said "fill it up lad" so I put a scoop of chips on his plate and he just stood there looking at me, it was at this point that I was told by the screw, who a short while earlier had given me the '1 scoop' order "hurry up chuck loads on for him you heard the man"! Well that just showed me that Paul Sykes got what he wanted when he wanted.

There was an almighty clash between Paul Sykes and ex-boxer from Newcastle Freddie Mills (aka 'mad Fred the head') in Durham in 1986. On this occasion, they were bringing Freddie back up to the wing from the Segregation Unit and as soon as Sykes set eyes on Fred he ambushed him and gave him a heavy whack with a murderous right hand that would have knocked a wall down, there was a hellish brawl. Fred managed to get back up from the punch and rugby tackled Sykesy to the ground, it was at that moment that around a dozen officers broke the fight up and locked us all up and closed the prison down.

Sykesy and Freddie hated each other with a passion perhaps it was because Freddie considered himself to be the top dog in Durham until Sykesy came in and took that title from him, it was almost like they battled to be the alpha male. They knew each other on the out but only clashed upon being in close proximity; Sykes definitely instigated it all that day though.

I don't mind admitting that I was terrified of Sykes at that time as I was only a young lad and I'd heard all the stories about Paul Sykes raping people like me, whether they were made up or not I don't know but I wasn't going to chance it so I always tried to keep my distance from him. He'd always be striding around very moody looking, almost like a caged tiger, you couldn't trust him not to attack you over nothing at all. It wasn't just me that tried to keep out of his way the mates that I had in there were also fearful of him.

Sykesy would walk around completely fearless and he didn't need any back up to strut around like he did with the cloud of menace that hung around him when it wasn't even his 'local' Jail either, well it took some brass neck to say the least.

People would slag him behind his back but never to his face, not if they valued their teeth anyway. When Paul Sykes came on the landing everybody would be on edge even the screws. There was a different atmosphere when Sykes was behind his door though people could be a little more relaxed.

Some days at dinner if Paul wasn't happy with his food then the

Prison Officers would take it back to the kitchen and get him what he wanted, they knew it was better to give him what he wanted because the alternative was going to take 10 Prison officers to get him back to his cell.

I know when Sykes attacked Freddie Mills and he was put in segregation the wing was a less nervous place to be than when Paul was around. He would often spend time in segregation and depending on where you were in the prison you could hear him kicking the cell door for hours upon hours.

One of the most monstrous stories that was linked to Paul Sykes was 'the baccy game', rumour had it that Paul would say to a YP "if you can climb through that wooden chair there you can win yourself an ounce of baccy", so the kid would have a go at it then when they were half way through the chair rendering themselves defenceless Paul would then steam in and rape these young lads, I don't know how true that is but it would be something that I would hear so many times over the years. Nobody would call Paul a sex case to his face but it was certainly said behind Paul's back!

Back in the days you were only let out of your cell twice a week on a night time but you'd hear Paul trying to kick holes in his cell door demanding to be out so the screws would let him out for half an hour just to keep him happy, he certainly got away with more than most prisoners would.

Even when I was in Frankland or Armley Paul would be spoken about even though he wasn't in there, his name and reputation struck fear into some of the hardest of inmates.

# MARK SZEDZIELARZ

Mark Szedzielarz is now 51 years old and for the last 16 years has lived in Australia. Mark grew up in Normanton and spent a few years on the doors of Wakefield's nightclubs earning a living.

I hope Mark doesn't mind me writing this but from looking at his old photo's he certainly wasn't your average looking doorman any more than Oscar De La Hoya is your average looking boxer! It is clear to see why he also earnt a living from modelling and being a male stripper. I can see why he was hired to work the doors, not only did he keep himself in shape and was clean living but he obviously provided eye candy for the ladies too.

\*　　　\*　　　\*　　　\*

I first heard about Paul Sykes in 1981 because of a massive brawl he'd had with a gang called 'The Street House Gang'. They were a very close-knit gang and very active in violence, they used to go fighting at football matches that kind of stuff.

I heard one night that Paul had had one almighty rumble in The Strafford Pub in Wakefield. The word on the street was that this man Paul Sykes had taken the full team of 'The Street House Gang' on, like all fifteen to twenty of them. Rumour had it that Paul wouldn't go down even though they were hitting him with Pool cues and Pool balls in socks, they surrounded him like pack animals but he wouldn't give in. The stories that I heard from people who were there were that Paul held his own with the lot of them although he was slightly worse for wear.

I got to meet him for the first time in Roof Top Gardens in the later months of 1989 and he'd just been released from Prison. I remember all the door staff team being told that Paul Sykes was on the premises so we all needed to be extra vigilant. I entered the seating area where Paul was and I noticed this huge figure sprawled across the settee, he had about six or seven young lads sat around him all wide eyed and hanging on his every word as he told them stories about his life. As it was the end of the night and closing time I walked over to Paul and his eager audience and spoke to them politely saying "excuse me Gents can you drink up now and make your way to the exit door please". I could see the look on these impressionable young lads faces, sneering almost, you could tell they were thinking 'oh you're gonna try and move Paul Sykes are ya'. Paul sat up slightly and on looking me up and down said to me "oh I'd have had some fun with you in the nick pretty boy", I said to him "you wouldn't have got near me mate" he then asked me how long I had been doing my job, I told him it was four years now, he then said to me "you must be good at your job, you haven't a mark on ya" with that he turned to his young groupies and told them "come on lads we better move off" and off he went quietly to Casanova's which was next door.

Casanova's used to attract quite a few well-known faces. I would see Dennis Flint dancing in there among a group of ladies, he would have his shirt undone right down to the last button and he had a massive gold Krugerrand on his chest, solid gold, like a big sun, although Dennis' tan was as golden as his Krugerrand! Jim Bowen, Jane McDonald even George Michael & Andrew Ridgeley have all been to Casanova's, I remember knocking back the Leeds Utd team because they had jeans on! These people would be in the VIP section, somewhere Paul was never to go himself, he was lucky if he managed to keep himself in the building!

Often some of the doormen were too afraid to say no to him and they'd let him in, then I would be left with the problem of getting him out, maybe it was because he had taken a shine to me or perhaps I didn't look menacing enough but he always went quietly when I asked him to, no drama's or anything. I recall one night when he said to me "you can escort me out but not that evil bastard there" whilst he was pointing to an ex doorman called Richard Brown. Richard was only slim with a beard but he could fight like hell he was a 4th Dan Black belt in Karate. I was told that Richard had had a real tear up with Paul the week before when Paul wasn't drunk. Richard had stood up to Paul so Paul was very wary of him after that. I knew Richard could look after himself, I'd seen him drop into the splits and hit people in the groin like Jean Claude Van Damme! I'd have been very interested to see what had gone on with them two the week before that's for sure.

Another time in Casanova's Paul had been let in and I had been given the grand job of asking Paul to leave, which I did. Paul as usual, with me at least, didn't cause any aggro. I took him to the foyer of the club and said, "listen Paul if you behave you can sit in the front entrance and have a drink" well this really pleased him so he gave me his money and off I went to get him a pint of lager. I'd caused myself a bit of a problem though as I spent a fair bit of time that night moving people on from the front of the club because a few young lads wanted to sit in the foyer with Paul and listen to his tales. At the end of the night he thanked me for it and shook my hand and off he went, no trouble at all.

A little while after that I took my Stepson up to Lupset Boys Club where Paul was training the kids. He would push them boys bloody hard and you could see that Paul enjoyed it all. He was a strict disciplinarian, if only he had put far more energy into that club it could have gone a long way but of course Paul Sykes liked to do what Paul Sykes liked to do, even though he had a lot of backers financially in that gym, like Paul Summers and Dennis Flint.

Paul Sykes had all the talent in the world, except the talent of knowing how to use his talent! You just can't help somebody who doesn't want to be helped or doesn't think they need to be helped.

# KENNY WILLIAMS

Kenny Williams grew up on the Eastmoor Estate and is 54 now. Kenny has been a bouncer for 31 years and now owns his own Door Supervision company in Wakefield. I thought Kenny may have had some knowledge of Paul Sykes for obvious reasons. Here is what Kenny could tell me about Paul.

*     *     *     *

I knew Paul Sykes when I was just a school boy, around the age of 14/15 and like every lad in Wakefield we all knew of him. Paul was known for beating people up and I suppose he was a bit of a celebrity to the young impressionable schoolboys such as myself. Sometimes we'd see him about then he'd disappear for X amount of time but even when he was absent because he was on his jollies in the nick, his name was still banded about a lot.

The first time I would meet Paul would be at the back end of the 1970's when Paul was in the prime of his life and at the top of his game in boxing. I'd bump into him in Norman Cunliffe's second hand shop on Parklodge Lane on the Eastmoor Estate. Us kids used to hang around the shops there and sometimes we'd go in Normans shop if he let us. Paul was a good friend of Norman's. This day, we were in Norman's shop when Paul walked in with his training bag slung over his shoulder as he'd just finished training, when not far behind him came in this Asian fella and he had a big brown leather jacket on, Paul saw him and marched up to him and said, "Get my leather jacket off ya black bastard", all us kids just froze we were shitting ourselves that something was gonna kick off. The Asian fella turns around and said, "You sold it to me last night in the club". It turns out that Paul had been pissed the night before and sold his jacket on to this poor bloke. He was standing his ground and wouldn't give Paul the jacket back so Paul ended up giving him a right hander and knocking this unfortunate guy out! On his way out of the shop, Paul came up to our group of lads and said, "Don't be fucking saying owt, you've never seen owt right!".

I left the shop shortly after Paul and had to walk the same way he had gone and somehow, completely unintentionally, I caught him up and we ended up walking together. As we got a bit along the road Paul said to me "Ere kid hold this for me" it was his sports bag, he was checking his right hand and I could see he had badly marked it, he looked at me with a furrowed brow and said, "I think I hit that paki a little bit too hard". We set off walking again and he started asking me questions about what I did with my time and would I like to take up boxing, but to be honest all I was thinking about was how I could get away from him asap. In the end, I made my excuses and turned off down a corner, I didn't need to be down that way but I was in a hurry to be out of his company.

I would go on to see Paul quite a lot in Norman's shop and he used to have a craic with us kids, we weren't really frightened of him because he always seemed a bit of a laugh as he would take the piss out of anyone that might be passing by. He had the same mentality as us really, you'd have thought he was of a similar age to us if you were just to hear him. He'd say to us "If anyone says owt to you young lads you just let me know and I'll right em" so, for this reason alone a lot of kids in Wakefield idolised him, he was a professional boxer at the time too and often made the papers most weeks. Many years later I would get to know Paul and become much more familiar with him and this time not so friendly!

I spent nine years on The Wine Lodge door (now Montgomery's) and we never ever let him in. This was throughout the 90's, Paul was turned away every single time and his parting shot would be to threaten us all, he always said to me "I thought you were my mate" because he recognised me but I just used to explain to him "It's not us Paul it's the Landlords" as they all knew that if we let Paul in he'd be a handful. He'd take up a lot of manpower when he tried to get in as they'd usually only be myself and a guy called Vinny on the door but when we saw Paul coming up the street we had to radio for another two to keep him at bay!

Paul never swung any punches at me whilst I worked on the doors there but he would shout "Cunts" at us when he'd given up hope of getting in. I thought myself fortunate as I'd heard plenty of stories of him knocking door staff out for them not letting him in, but he'd shout "Grass" and "I'll fucking find ya" that was stuff we heard quite often when he was departing. Nobody ever grassed him to the law to my knowledge but it was something he liked to say.

Many years later I would get to know Paul inside the walls of a few different prisons and from what I saw of him in prison I would definitely say he was a bully!

There were a few times I saw Paul having disagreements with people and he stroked a few even if they said to him that they weren't looking for any trouble, he wasn't bothered, he didn't fuck around.

One night in Heppy's nightclub in Wakefield it was all going off and Paul was at the centre of it. The bouncers had let him in but now they wanted him out and he wasn't prepared to oblige. The doormen had all been too afraid to approach him so they had no alternative but to call the police. The Police arrived and circled him but before they managed to overpower him he did a good job of catching a few coppers with right hand left hooks!

Bernard Handlin, "No teeth" Tony and Pete Riley were on the door, all quite capable men but Paul was just so wild and powerful the only way to get Paul out of the club that night was with the dogs and the riot squad.

I saw Paul in Armley in 1977 when I was a YP, he was in for a botched robbery attempt that he'd carried out with an accomplice. This was the last sentence he did before giving it a go as a pro boxer. All the screws were scared stiff of him and they just wanted him right out of the way, he did most of that sentence in the block (solitary), it made it easier for them.

I then came across him again in Strangeways in 1981 after his boxing career had finished. While Paul was in there he had some problems with this Irish guy, he was very small but stocky and powerful and he wouldn't back down from Paul. Every single time they crossed paths they fought. You'd have thought that this Irish guy and Paul's friend Delroy Showers were made from the same mould, he was also very well respected in prison and nobody messed with him. When Paul wasn't in the block Paul and Delroy would always be together.

The last time I saw Paul in prison was in Armley in 2005, he didn't have long left after that as it turns out. People were knocking him over a lot on the landings. He'd arrived in Armley from living on the streets drinking Special Brew every day, he was frail and you could tell he wasn't the same man he once had been as he didn't have the fear factor about him that he'd once had. He had just given up looking after himself. Even whilst he was in prison, with washing facilities, clean laundry and three meals a day he still managed to look like a bum and scruffy.

You'll find a lot of people like him in prisons i.e. druggies and alcoholics and he just looked like one of them. On previous occasions Paul Sykes had practically lived in the prison gym but not in 2005, he never went near it.

Paul was placed in segregation a lot in 2005 only this time it was for his own safety not the safety of others, it was very sad to see him like this. When I'd first come across him in Prison in 1977 he had stood out from everyone else in that prison. Paul walked tall and walked alone and he made up his own rules to live by he didn't care about anyone else's rules. Then in 2005 he just wanted to keep a low profile and blend in with the rest of the prison population.

For years the stories of him attacking the young YP's were doing the rounds on the prison grapevine, his sayings were folklore "We can do it my way or the hard way" was something he would be heard to say quite frequently. I heard the other rumours about him too but I couldn't say whether these were true or not. I imagine his friend Delroy Showers would be the person to ask about that.

The last time I ever saw Paul was on a bench in Wakefield town, he was sat drinking Special Brew, he shouted me over and shook my hand.

He never asked me for anything but I remember just being so thrown that a human being could become as lost as he had become. I'm not making excuses for the guy but I do think he was misunderstood I really do. I mean there was a bloke who could have done loads with this life when he'd finished boxing. He could have opened a boxing club for kids and they'd have flocked to him.

If you took the time to speak with him you'd soon find out that there wasn't much that he didn't know something about, but obviously on the downside he was a very violent man on occasions.

Paul Sykes will never be forgotten in Wakefield, certainly not within my lifetime. I'll never forget the bloke. He was a man in our city and he was always up to something that's just what he was like. He was a one off and I'm sure they'll be other people in this book that will have said the same thing. Another thing I will say that's been said before and will be said again is that he was mentally ill, although he tried very hard to cover it up.

There were so many bad things that Paul did whilst he was drunk and some people would say he was only violent after a drink but I know of him hitting many people while he was stone cold sober just because he didn't like something that they had said. Just like the Asian guy I told you about that he knocked out in Norman Cunliffe's shop that day. Norman was bigger than Paul but was built like a matchstick and Paul would bully Norman. I remember a day that Paul had had a go at Norman and Paul Burke sorted Paul out. Nobody could believe it but apparently, they'd had a fight and Burkey won! Burkey would be a fabulous man to speak to about Paul Sykes. Burkey and Sykesy were really good mates.

At the end of his life there was a group of young kids that would give him a crack almost on a daily basis, they had no respect for who he once was. If anyone from his generation had gone and hit him while he was a down and out we wouldn't have got brownie points we'd have just looked like twats. Those kids wouldn't have faced him in his day so why do it then when he was frail and vulnerable. It was all so very sad.

*"I was an 18-year-old in the body of a man of 31"*

**-P Sykes**

\*On his release from prison in 1977

# TOMMY HARRISON

As you will be aware if you've read Unfinished Agony, I grew up in the fine town of Middlesbrough in an area called Berwick Hills, also affectionately known as Beverly Hills! For any football fans reading this, Berwick Hills is also the area where the fiery headed Philip Stamp who played for Middlesbrough and Hearts of Midlothian hails from.

I've always been aware of Tommy Harrison's name since I was around 12 years of age, the reason behind that I'm not sure of but maybe it was because it was a name brandished about around the Middlesbrough boxing scene. He is very well respected and very well connected in the Teesside area.

I knew about Paul's great love for Teesside from John and Tony Spensley who, of course, had chapters in the first book but I had never really got the connection with Paul Sykes and Middlesbrough's Mr Big until I spent a bit of time in the company of the charismatic Delroy Showers. Delroy asked me if I'd contacted Tommy Harrison. It threw me a little as I was wondering how Delroy had heard of Tommy, it is a small world indeed!

Delroy told me about his close friendship with Tommy and of the travels they'd had to Paris and Pakistan.

My only dilemma now was how was I going to get hold of Tommy Harrison's phone number and how was I going to persuade him to give me the time of day and speak to me. I eventually and gratefully got a number for Tommy from an ex-boxer friend of mine in Middlesbrough called Tony Robbo, "Here Jamie try that number" was the message I got from Tony.

I put on my best telephone voice and phoned Tommy, trying to sound like a total professional I hit him with the 'Sykes bomb', there was a long pause, too long, I started to feel a bit uncomfortable, then Tommy said, "Paul Sykes?" then another long pause, had I dropped a clanger here, were they deadly enemies or the best of mates? I'm sure my relief was obvious even down the phone when I heard Tommy eventually say, "Very good friend of mine was Paul Sykes" and his tone softened, "I'll meet you outside Isaac Wilson's tomorrow 11.30am Son, don't be late" was what he said.

The next day I was there nice and early and Tommy arrived very smartly dressed with an old trusted friend of his of 45 years Buster Atkinson and although we had decided to meet outside the pub Tommy told me that he hadn't drank since the funeral of his Son Lee Harrison. Tommy's son Lee was another well-known and well-liked face on Teesside who tragically had been found dead the year before in Lebanon in very suspicious circumstances. Tommy told me his son was murdered but it had been made to look like a suicide. Tommy is 74 now but he said he will never stop fighting to get justice for Lee.

We decided to find somewhere where we would have some peace and quiet so Tommy, Buster and I went to Gordon Murphy's café in North Ormesby called Norman Baum's and we had a cuppa and a chat.

\*       \*       \*       \*

I first heard about Paul Sykes when I was in Durham nick in 1966. There was a lot of talk about this big rough lad who was a boxer, at the time Paul would have only been 20 years old but he'd built up an awesome reputation as a fighter. The word around was that although he was continually fighting the system he was a very intelligent man along with it.

I wouldn't meet Paul until the mid 1970's though when he came to my house with his friends Ronnie Threlfall and Delroy Showers for a business meeting on certain projects in different countries. I shook his massive hands and I must say I liked him instantly. Paul was constantly telling jokes that day and I liked a laugh.

I got to know Paul Sykes over many years and I found him to be a great guy. I always only speak as I find, we always got on and I can only talk well of him from my personal experience of being in his company. Over the years I've read all kinds of rubbish written about him by people who'd never even met the man. Throughout all the times I was in his company, whether it be in my home, at his house or just around Lupset I was always very impressed by his behaviour. The only time I ever saw Paul strike someone was in The Malt Shovel in Wakefield and the guy deserved it, the guy was really trying his luck with Paul and next thing 'boom boom' two punches and the fella was down end of story. Paul was in the right on that occasion.

Paul absolutely loved Middlesbrough and he'd visit here a lot. I usually met him every time he came through. I knew sometimes that he was coming to do debt collecting work, but I never got involved in that, that wasn't my game, being a bailiff.

Paul would ask me who certain people in the Middlesbrough area were and I knew that he was headhunting. One thing about Paul Sykes that I'd like to say is that he was a very clever man, this was down mostly to the studying he did whilst in prison, he didn't waste his time reading nonsense and he studied the rule books about the prison system, he knew his rights!

Sometime around the early 1990's I had a fall out with a Middlesbrough club owner, this club owner got in touch with Charlie Kray to get hold of Alex Steen as he knew he would have contact details for Paul Sykes as there was "A problem" in Middlesbrough. Apparently, the club owner had put a contract out on me for £4,000. Well, I'd heard about this and I contacted both Charlie Kray and Alex Steen and said, "I'm the problem what are you gonna do?". I don't think they realised I knew Paul so I just told them that if he comes up he comes up.

So, in October 1989 on the night of Glenn McCrory's fight versus Siza Makathini at the Eston Sports Academy, which John Spensley promoted, Paul Sykes walks in, he had only been out of prison a month. My son Lee and many of his friends were there. Paul made a bee line for our Lee and asked him "Is yer Dad in?" Our Lee and many of his mates were all carrying coshes that night just in case something started to go off but Paul said, "I haven't come for any trouble with your Dad, he's a friend of mine". Paul found me and put his arms out to embrace me and we had a great night that night along with some very famous names, Jack Charlton was there, Tommy Miller and Matt Murray also.

When Paul and I had chance to speak he told me the details about what he'd been briefed. He said, "I'll go see that fucking club owner myself" and rumour has it that Paul did visit the club owner and he happily relieved him of the 4k he'd offered him to deal with me!

On one occasion when Paul came to Middlesbrough he told me about how he was going to write this book called Sweet Agony. I had a clothes shop in Guisborough at the time and he visited me there, he'd called in for a cuppa and I asked him if he needed any money to make his book happen, he said he did so I gave him a couple of hundred quid, when he visited again I gave him a bit more.

A year later I would see Paul, by total accident in Blackpool, he was sat in the Buckstead Manor and I was there having a meeting with a firm from Blackpool. I was chatting away then I heard this booming voice say, "Now then" I turned to see Paul Sykes stood there with Ronnie Threfall. The meeting was completely by chance and he told me times were hard, I offered him £100 and Paul laughed "Ere here's your £100 and £100 for yourself" I asked him if he'd robbed a bank! He told me "I haven't forgotten about the money you gave me for my book Tommy" but I told him that I had given him that because I wanted to give him it, he said "Nah you're a straight lad, there ya go". That was the last time I would ever speak to Paul in person and that was in 1992, I would speak to him on the phone many times after that though. I lost contact with Paul for many years, I spent so much time in Africa and then I went to prison in 2004 on a nine-year sentence so it was hard to keep in touch.

The end of Paul Sykes' life saddens me greatly, if he'd have picked up the phone I'd have helped him with a few quid he should have known that, he was my pal and I wouldn't have seen him living like that, money is only a tool isn't it?

Paul Sykes didn't have a mentor to guide him because he thought he was the clever one, he should have stuck at boxing but of course he chose the wrong path.

Paul would sit and listen to you, but if he had it in his head to do something it had to be done. I used to say to him "What have you got to prove Paul?" I used to say that to the Duff (Legendary Teesside hard man Lee Duffy) too but neither of them would listen to anyone.

I found Paul Sykes to be a lovely lad and he was always very honest and genuine with me. Paul loved being in Middlesbrough but he wasn't as well-known as he was in his home town of Wakefield. People in Middlesbrough knew him well enough though, that if you're going to cause trouble with Paul Sykes you were going to get hurt

# DAVID FLINT

Grandson of Dennis Flint RIP


The documentary Paul Sykes at Large had its fair share of characters in it other than Paul Sykes.

For my first book, Unfinished Agony, I spoke to Kenny the Tailor who was a favourite of mine and whilst writing this book I've had the pleasure of meeting Delroy Showers who is a fascinating man, but someone who has always intrigued me is the charismatic Dennis Flint. It saddened me greatly therefore to learn that Dennis Flint passed away on the 5th of September 2001. The Yorkshire Post did a big piece in their paper when Dennis died, that's how well known he was.

Although I would never get the opportunity to speak with Dennis I was elated to discover that his Grandson David was happy to speak to me about his Grandfather.

I sat back and listened intently as David told me about his unique Grandfather and his Grandfathers pal Paul Sykes.

*       *       *       *

I'm 41 years old and I grew up in Wakefield, I've lived in Sandal, Horbury, Durkar, Kettlethorpe, Heath Common, Agbrigg, Peacock, Flanshaw, Lupset, and Outwood. I now live in Kirklees and I am married with three children, my professional title is David Flint BSc MBCS and I have worked as an I.T. Professional for nearly twenty years.

Everyone in Wakefield knew my Grandad Dennis Flint, in fact when the producers of the First Tuesday documentary about Paul Sykes had finished making it, they also wanted to make a documentary about my Grandfather Dennis. I don't know the reason why the Documentary on

Dennis was never made but it was something that people talked about for many years to come, in fact people still mention it now, especially as the First Tuesday "Paul Sykes at Large" video is now on YouTube, people quite often say they should have done another follow-up Documentary and regularly say "they should have done one about your Grandad".

Sometimes when I was at Primary School my Dad would drop me off in Rolls-Royce's and other expensive cars and from my earliest memories I can remember everywhere you would go in Wakefield people would say "are you related to Dennis Flint", there was always a lot of interest in Dennis as he was known to live in a Massive Mansion on Heath Common, drive expensive cars such as Rolls-Royce's and people were always interested in him and what he was doing, in fact, people still ask the same questions today as he was one of the true characters of Wakefield.

My family were very close when I was born and my Dad and Dennis wanted to name me "Dennis" but my Mum refused, Dennis pleaded with my Mum and said that if I was named Dennis that I'd never want for anything but my Mum wouldn't budge and went and registered me as "David" before anyone else got the chance, otherwise I would have been another Dennis Flint, well in name anyway!

One of my earliest childhood memories is going on holiday with Dennis and my Grandma Alice when I was about 3 years old, and we went to Land's End in Cornwall, I remember enjoying the holiday and I still quite often go to Cornwall as it is a lovely part of the Country and my Nana Audrey lives in Truro.

Although Dennis was my Grandad, I always referred to him as "Dennis" and there is a reason for that, but that is another story. I have many childhood memories of Dennis as I was growing up and one memory that stands out, in particular, was when I was about 12 years old and I had started playing Golf at school and Dennis insisted that I could borrow his Ping Golf Clubs and use them, but I remember my Uncle Mark said I didn't need them and he got me some Dunlop or Slazenger Clubs instead, by the way, my Uncle Mark was a Professional Golfer, he used to teach from the age of 15 years and I believe he had a handicap of three and I know he was well known in the field of Golf when I was younger and both Dennis and my Grandma Alice were both very proficient and keen Golfers.

Unfortunately, as Families do fall out from time to time there were times when people may not speak within the family. There was a big bust up with Dennis and my Dad when I was about 13 years old and they didn't really speak properly for the best part of ten years, it made it awkward when I would see him in town. Quite often he would pull over in his expensive cars and he'd be looking over to speak to me but out of sheer loyalty to my Father, I would often ignore him. I remember one occasion when the whole school walked down Northgate from QEGS to Wakefield Cathedral, it was probably Foundation Day or something and Dennis had seen me and stopped at the side of the road in his bright red Rolls-Royce and everyone was commenting saying "wow, have you seen the Roller" but I just walked past and ignored him and to be fair it is something I quite often feel bad about to this day, as Dennis was always very proud of all his family.

Growing up my Dad, Steven was a massive boxing fan, and I regularly used to watch the box set of the Rocky films, as a child and I used to watch all the fights at the time with my Dad such as:- Eubank, Benn, Watson, Bruno, Hearns, Hagler, Spinks, one of my Dad's all-time favourite boxers was Barry McGuigan and like many from my generation I watched the rise of Tyson as he walked through the Heavyweight Division and I remember the late nights from the early days of Pay-per-View stopping up to watch the Tyson fights. When I was about nineteen I also used to go watch Steve Tuckett, Bob's son, fight Professionally, usually at the Queens Hotel in Leeds but also in Sheffield where I saw Herol Bomber Graham, and also other places as a few of my mates were also well into boxing. In fact a few years ago I had lost touch with an old school friend, Stuart Pywell and it was about seven years ago and I had managed to get his mobile number so I gave him a ring and he said "I can't talk now Dave, I'm just about to meet Mike Tyson", he did however ring me back and say that he thought afterwards that it sounded like a ludicrous excuse but he had in fact just met Mike Tyson when he was doing the Charity Events and After Dinner Speeches, in fact, he was pleased to tell me that he had just won an auction and bought a pair of Iron Mike's Boxing Gloves and that they had just drawn the Charity Raffle and he had just won a brand new motorcycle.

I don't know if it would be right to draw parallels at this stage between Mike Tyson and Paul Sykes but in my opinion people respect Mike Tyson in much the same way that they respect Paul Sykes, for his incredible boxing ability and they choose to put the fact that he is a convicted rapist to the back of their minds. Perhaps people also realise the hassle that Tyson has gone through, perhaps he was not guilty of what he has been accused of, and I feel the same could be said about Paul Sykes, because unless we were actually there, then nobody knows what really happened on the day, nobody knows what is added through poetic license, but like you say Paul Sykes did happen and he did draw attention whilst he was alive, and he is still drawing attention now because one thing for sure is he was a character and a complete one off.

Paul Sykes was a name that I heard many times as a child growing up but I never really put a face to the name until about 1990 when the First Tuesday "Paul Sykes at Large" Documentary aired on ITV and bearing in mind at the time there were only four channels on TV, it seemed that every man and his dog had seen the Documentary, although I didn't as I was probably at Karate or something. Regardless of me not seeing it when it aired on TV, it was the talk of the town the next day, especially at school. I attended Queen Elizabeth's Grammar School and my first real memory of Paul Sykes was the next day at school, everyone was talking about it, even the school teachers were chatting about it. I had a lot of people coming up to me saying that they couldn't believe how cool my Grandfather was, there were even a few that asked if I would speak to my Grandad and Paul Sykes and get them to collect debts for their father's! I remember that day wondering what all the commotion was about and when I got home that night from school we had it on VHS and I watched the Documentary so at least I was on the same page as everybody else in Wakefield. I can understand why the Documentary is a cult classic and why it is considered comedy gold as it is full of one-liners that people recite after watching it, and it is what it is, it is a very entertaining programme and people to this day will say to me "when you're sober....etc".

I think one of the positives to draw upon from the Documentary is that when Paul made an attempt to use his brain rather than his brawn and took to writing a book then it was Dennis that backed him from a business point of view, I also genuinely believe Dennis was a positive influence on Paul as "Sykesy" needed somebody who could handle him and keep him in line just like it says in the documentary "I don't like you drinking beer and smoking roll ups, okay, when you're sober, you're an educated man, but when you are drunk you're a fucking maniac" and I would stand by this statement that Dennis made and feel that obviously if Paul had 20 GCSE's, 8 A Levels, a Degree, read three books a week and served 21 years then he had to have a vast knowledge and certainly was an educated man, this combined with his lightning fast wit and gift of the gab made him a character.

Another person I found interesting when I was younger was Jimmy Boyle, hence why I asked if you were related to him, as I read his book "A Sense of Freedom" when I was about twelve years old and as well as being the first book of that Genre that I read, it really did leave an impression on me as I was a young lad, especially the fact that Boyle had turned his life around against all odds in order to become a successful Author, something that perhaps Paul Sykes could have developed further himself if he hadn't slipped into the downward spiral of drink and drugs.

After the documentary had been and gone I heard Paul Sykes had been down Waldorf Way, where my Dad, Uncle Mark, and Dennis had garages and he was selling his book, Sweet Agony and I heard he had been into all the other businesses down Waldorf Way and everywhere else in the area and was just walking into places and saying, 'stop what you're doing because you have got to buy my book' but funnily enough they all did just as he said, and they all bought copies.

Paul Sykes used to be friends with a guy called Dave Cooling but they used to call him Cuckoo, I suppose the clue is in the name as to why they called him that, but Paul and Cuckoo fell out and to avoid seeing Paul, Cuckoo moved literally to the other side of the world, Australia, he moved all that way because he was that afraid of Paul. Paul Sykes and Cuckoo had been best friends at some point but had a big fall out and I first met Dave (Cuckoo) when I was about 14 years old and knew him for many years, to be honest, he was very much like Paul Sykes in his looks and mannerisms, he too was very quick witted, very intelligent and could change in a heartbeat from laughing to scowling and then back to laughing again, he was a good bloke and very entertaining and we had a few laughs together.

When I was about 15 years old, I saw Paul Sykes when he came into Bourbon Street nightclub, it was the lowest class of nightclub in Wakefield at the time, it had the typical sticky carpets and it was just an absolute dive. On this occasion, I looked up from the dance floor as I could see that there was a load of commotion going on and there were bouncer's everywhere. In amongst them stood Paul Sykes and two women, one on each arm and I remember thinking at the time he looked massive. Paul walked right in and straight through the bouncers who were moving out of the way, and for a moment the atmosphere in the nightclub dropped, you'd have thought King Kong was trying to make his way in, the way people were trying to get out of his way. Paul walked over to a table near the entrance and sat down making himself comfortable with his two girlfriends. He can't have been there any more than 5 or 10 minutes when two bouncers came over with carrier bags full of bottles and cans and gave them to Paul. Paul picked up his of booze and went on his merry way with these two girls. This was really a bargaining tool from the club for Paul to go elsewhere without a fuss, here's £100 worth of drink if you go somewhere else and leave us all alone but it was completely out of the ordinary to see bouncers just let somebody, especially just one man, just walk in and do as he pleased without them trying to do anything about it.

Even though Paul was 6ft 3 ½ inches he always seemed even bigger than that, he was very imposing, he had really broad shoulders and at 6ft 3 and sixteen stone by today's standards that might not appear "big" but he really had a presence and he was a big man, a very big man. He was laughing and joking when he walked into Bourbon Street but it didn't matter if he had a smile on his face there was always an aura of menace about him and this is probably why the bouncers just didn't want to upset him even though they outnumbered him, it was more trouble than it was worth. He would get this look on his face, his mood could change in one tenth of a second and he'd go from laughing to scowling and looking seriously scary in the click of a finger.

When I was sixteen, I would bump into Paul again at Wakefield Magistrates Court. I was there supporting my Nana Audrey as she had been injured in a serious fall and I was there as a witness to what had happened, coincidentally this was my first experience of the corruption in Wakefield as the representatives from Wakefield Council stood up in Court and lied terribly under Oath, I was disgusted. While we were waiting to go into court Paul was there and he started talking to us. Paul was polite, articulate and very quick witted, he was the ideal company sat waiting in a dreary court house wanting to pass the time, he was a very entertaining man, he was discussing a wide array of topics such as a Farmer from Barnsley who had perfected a way to extract methane gas from waste and was making money from it as a fuel source and stating that it confirmed what he had heard, "that where there's muck, there's brass!". When it came to discussing my Grandfather, Dennis, Paul told me how much he loved and respected Dennis and thought really very highly of him as a trusted friend. By the way, Paul used to defend himself in the Magistrates Court rather than using solicitors in those days.

When I was about seventeen I was at my lifelong best friend, Sean Bailey's house at 3 Gissing Road on Lupset, where Sean had lived for about ten years and it was more or less opposite where Paul Sykes lived. I remember we were in Sean's house and all of sudden there was loads of commotion, shouting, police sirens etc, so we both ran outside into the street to see what was happening and about a hundred yards away Paul Sykes was sat on the kerb surrounded by police cars. Sean said "come on it's Sykesy, let's go in before he sees us", as Paul was known to get drunk and cause merry mayhem and at times be completely out of control, I said "no, I want to see what's happening", so I stood and watched for probably the best part of an hour. On this occasion Paul was sat on the kerb just outside the entrance to Jubilee Hall and the "Reck" as the playground was known, and he had a bag of booze at the side of him and was well and truly pissed out of his head, and to start with there were three police cars surrounding him but every time a police officer tried to open a car door he would jump to his feet in Nano-seconds and shout at them "Get back in that fucking car or else …." and surprisingly they did. Eventually there were about six police cars there and God knows how many police officers and this situation just went on and on as Paul insisted he was not going anywhere with the police officers, and they were too frightened to get out of their cars, like I say this standoff went on for the best part of an hour until Paul seemed to have sobered up enough to jump up one final time to announce that he was bored and he wasn't playing anymore and he was going to go sleep it off and at that point he went off in to the Reck where Jubilee Hall is and the police didn't seem to know what to do. I heard later that he had gone into the Reck and gone to sleep on his own accord to sleep it off, and it would seem that the police were happy for him to do this rather than having any confrontation, it did seem that they were quite powerless as no single officer wanted to be the first one to jump in and get a right hook.

Around that time when I was seventeen or eighteen I was in Sixth Form at Queen Elizabeth Grammar School doing my A Levels and I was becoming increasingly aware of the Police Harassment that Dennis, my Dad, and Mark would experience and as I was driving at that time and usually drove nice cars, I had an XR3 and Astra GTI and regularly used to borrow cars from my Dad such as BMW's and the like and I would get pulled by the police all the time, the thing is they didn't used to pull me because I had a light out on the car or anything they would stop me and be laughing as my name would come up on the PNC and they would ask if I was related to Dennis and they would be laughing and making jibes, asking questions about my family such as "have your Dad and Dennis been fighting recently" and I used to have to ask them if that is all they wanted and if so let them know that I would be going on my way but to be honest for the police it was like a little bit of sport just stopping me and harassing me in front of my friends, in other words really it was paramount to bullying using their position of authority to make my life difficult because of whose son or grandson I was. On one occasion the police officers were laughing and joking between themselves and one of the officers was telling the other this is Dennis Flints Grandson, and this particular copper didn't know who my Grandad was so the first copper described him as being "like Paul Sykes but with business acumen".

The thing is that Dennis was very well known around Wakefield and beyond, so as a young child growing up he was always known as being a "Medallion Man" because of the large flashy jewellery he used to wear, and this "fame" or "urban legend" status meant that many people considered him to be a Gangster, so this did actually come at a price because the police harassed my Dad, my Uncle and myself for many years to come, as if in some way to exact a vengeance that they thought that Dennis had got away with everything so they would target his children and children's children in a way to pay him back. Most people have to have a level of composure and restraint when those in authority choose to be wicked and evil because they know that they won't beat the system but Paul Sykes stood for something else, which meant to hell with the consequences and quite often he intimidated the people who abuse their positions of authority and what you need to understand is that Wakefield is not like other places, where there is a shortage of bobbies on the beat so to speak, the National Police Headquarters was based on Laburnum Road, the Police Training School was based at Bishopgarth, in fact, The Blackstone's Police Operational Handbook that is used Nationally was copyrighted to Bishopgarth, Wakefield. The thing is Wakefield is commonly referred to as being a Police State because of the number of overzealous new recruits that run around the streets, eager to get their first arrest, eager to use their weapons and generally all hyped up, and it is not a good thing to be on the receiving end of it. I would like to say that I have a genuine contempt for West Yorkshire Police, I have suffered police harassment in many forms for most of my life, as a child my Dad was targeted by the police because they "thought Dennis was a Criminal" and because they couldn't get to Dennis they would try and get to my Dad. As a child in primary school and you've got to realise that to me having a Grandad that had a Mansion was normal, having a Grandad that drove Rolls-Royce's was normal, my Dad dropping me off at school in expensive cars was normal, my Dad, my Uncle, my Grandad and many people I knew wore Rolex watches and again this was normal but I remember when I was about maybe six years old and Dennis was on Calendar News because a gang had broken into Heath House and beaten him up very badly because they were trying to rob him, I remember at the time how genuine this was, I remember speaking to Dennis about it in 1998 and he said it wouldn't happen again because he had a gun and he wouldn't think twice about shooting the next person that tried to break in and rob him. On balance, I do have friends whose parents are police officers, and for whom I have great respect and I have met police officers throughout my working life that have been very nice, amenable people but in my opinion, there are quite a few rotten apples in the barrel in Wakefield and this rot does spread. I remember Clive Harrison telling me about twenty years ago "It takes a lifetime to earn a good reputation and a second to lose it" and I think this applies equally well to the police in so much as when you take the time to realise that when you or your family are in trouble you automatically ring 999, and the police are the ones that quite often have to do a very difficult job, they are the people that you should be able to trust, but then when you experience the other side of it, when the police are no better than the people who they are locking up, then all that goes out of the window. I do remember one of my friends from school Jonathan Atkins, who by the way was a great lad, had told me after the First Tuesday Documentary that he hated Paul Sykes because his own Dad was a police officer and he had been on the bus upstairs, on his way home from work and Paul Sykes had attacked him and beaten him up just for being a copper, and my friend Jonathan was a genuine lad and I have no reason to believe that this isn't true. I do believe that Paul Sykes did bully the bullies, but I think from the stories that I have heard that he also indiscriminately bullied many people, young, old, vulnerable, so there are times when his love of violence is hard to justify.

As I mentioned before, my Dad, my Uncle Mark and Dennis all had garages on Waldorf Way as I was growing up and it was common for many people to visit the garage, especially characters from the Wakefield area and beyond, in fact quite often the Sales Office would be full of colourful people who would be entertaining and discussing many issues, although for the best part when I was younger me and Sean would be playing in or around the garage.

On one particular occasion, me and Sean were working on cars in the garage and it would have been around 1998 and when we went into the office it was packed full of people, my Uncle Mark was there and Paul Sykes was talking and keeping everybody entertained. It was around the time Paul had featured in FHM Magazine as "Britain's Hardest Man" and he started telling me about it as soon as I walked in to the Office, and he showed me the article and I looked, and asked "is it true", he turned quick as a flash, scowling and said "well I'm not Britain's fucking softest am I" and then just as quick, we both started laughing, at that point Mark said "David have a look at the size of his hands" and to that Paul lifted his hand up to mine , I had often heard that Paul Sykes "had hands like shovels", but to be honest you quite often have to separate the shit from the sweet corn when you hear things about people, but I can honestly say I have never seen a pair of hands as big in my life, they were twice as big as anybody's, and it was a very fair and accurate description, he did indeed have hands like shovels! I think Mark's next comment was "can you imagine getting whacked in the face by one of those", and to be honest it's not surprising he could hurt people so easily his fists were huge! It was a great day, Paul was very good company and he was there for a good few hours and constantly had people in stitches. I can remember a few of the quotes from the article like it stated that he was banned from all the local Taxi firms, he quoted "I've got nowt against Asians but if they want to live in my country the very least they should do is to give me a lift" and "I'd rather be the local drunk than the local nowt!" When he left I gave him a lift up to his brother in law's book shop that was on the corner of Wakefield Indoor Market and to be honest I don't think anybody could have had a bad word to say about Paul Sykes on that occasion, he was polite, entertaining and he loved being the centre of attention, he was a larger than life character.

Not long afterwards Paul came down again and this time he was pissed up, my family rented the Garage next door to Stockdale who had a Car Sales pitch and had a lot of lovely motors and they were all kept in pristine condition. Paul had cut across Stockdale's forecourt and on this particular day, Sykesy was paralytic and he jumped over a 2ft wall, doing so he tripped and fell into one of Stockdale's Cars, the front end, the bonnet, and wing were crushed and the car looked like it had been pranged, just by Paul falling on it drunk, it looked like it had been written off. When Paul picked himself up off the floor he was insistent that it was Stockdale's fault for leaving the car there and carrying on. It didn't even enter his mind that he was in the wrong! Paul Sykes was living proof that Jekyll and Hyde characters exist and on this occasion, Paul was a completely different person to the one he had been just a few days before. Nothing came of the damage he caused to the car, Stockdale, who I had heard was also a court Magistrate said he didn't want to ring the Police because he didn't want the rest of his cars damaging.

On another occasion I pulled up at to the garage on Waldorf Way shortly after Paul himself arrived, before I could get out of my car, I remember it was a red XR2 and I had just parked up and a guy called P.J. ran over frantically and jumped in my passenger seat shouting "quick, quick, DRIVE, Sykesy is here" I said "P.J. I've only just arrived and I've got stuff to do", he kept pleading with me "no, we've GOT TO GO, Sykesy is here" I told him again I wasn't going anywhere, and I got out of the car despite his pleas just to show him that I wasn't going anywhere, then P.J. jumped out of my car and ran away from them offices at lightning speed , straight down Waldorf Way. To be honest I didn't know what was going on and it just seemed to me that P.J. was off his head, I did know P.J. quite well at the time and he was always a really pleasant and polite person, never any bother and this really was very out of character for him, but to be fair he was acting odd and not making much sense, just shouting and screaming and he was in a mass panic. I didn't know it at the time, and didn't find out till later that while Sykesy had been locked up, P.J had apparently been knocking off Paul's ex, Cath and I was fully aware that P.J. was a Mormon, a member of the Church of the Latter Day Saints as he was always discussing it and being very evangelical whenever he visited the garage, but upon learning that it was P.J. that converted Cath to Christianity and they had been an item for quite a while it all started to make sense, I later heard that Paul had said that if he ever ran into P.J. he was going to kill him.

I went into the office anyway just as Sykesy had left and gone to a shady garage nearby and decided to make himself at home in their Sales Office instead, these guys were well known for taking deposits on cars and not returning them to customers and selling cars and if the customers returned they would tell them to "fuck off", the sort of garage that runs for three to six months and then disappears only to start up somewhere else under a new name and repeat the trail of ripping people off; it is people like this that give people in the Car Trade a bad name. Well, one of the guys was around 6ft 4 and 20 Stone, he used to strut his stuff thinking he was a right hard case, but on this occasion Sykesy had decided to keep them company and sat in their office terrorising them for hours, they were close to tears and they certainly hadn't had any customers all day! At one point the guy came to see my Uncle Mark to see if he could do anything about the situation as Paul had convinced himself that he would like to go to Spain and he had been telling the guys that they would have to pay for it, he was very drunk and just generally causing mayhem. Mark went round and brought Paul back round to the office at Waldorf and asked Paul what was going on and what the problem was, I remember Mark's friend Jamie Wrigglesworth was there and Paul stated that he wanted to go to Spain and wanted somebody to pay for it. With this Mark and Jamie agreed with him that it was a great idea, and that it sounded quite fair so they convinced him that from Wakefield to Spain the mid-point was about London, so they said that they would pay for him to get to London and he would have to get somebody there to pay for the other half of the journey, and Paul seemed quite amenable to the idea. So Mark and Jamie took Paul to Westgate Train Station and put him on the next train to London, they said afterwards that they had to get on with him and prop him up in the seat! To be fair the big bloke next door was known for being a crook and a bit of knob head, and was known to bully people, especially customers, but when he'd been given a bit of his own medicine, so to speak he couldn't handle it, and he was in a right old state, so I don't think people really had any sympathy for him. Whereas the damage to Stockdale's car did seem quite out of order, and just demonstrated the dark side to Paul's personality when he was pissed up and acting like a thug and a bully.

About a week later I was at the Garage and in the Office at Waldorf Way, there was just myself and my wife there, who was my girlfriend at the time, and Paul Sykes just turned up out of the blue. He wasn't drunk on this occasion and had come to pay my Uncle Mark back the train fare that he'd forked out to send Paul to London, Paul handed me £60 to pass on to my Uncle Mark and he seemed fine, he did insist a few times to make sure my Uncle received the money and I assured him I would pass it on to him. He asked me if I would like a smoke and if it was ok to stay and I said yes, but told him in no uncertain terms "as long as you don't ask to borrow a car", to which he replied innocently, "what do you mean, why can't I borrow a car", and I told him he knew damn well why, and that I was letting him know before he asked that the answer would be "no", and he did know exactly why he wasn't allowed to borrow cars but that's a different story. Anyway, everything was fine, we were chatting, he asked if I wanted a drink and I said no but he was welcome to if he wanted to, he asked my girlfriend if she would bob over to the shop and gets some cans, I think it was Special Brew which she got. At the time I was sat on the edge of one of the desks and Paul was sat in the corner of the office and when my girlfriend came back he insulted her and she ran out of the office and slammed the door shut, at that point I jumped up in a split second, threw some items at him and was stood over Paul and I went ballistic, I told him "I don't give a fuck who you think you are, get your stuff and fuck off" I was fuming and I totally lost it, Paul, on the other hand, was perfectly calm, his attitude totally changed, he apologised and looked very sincere, he asked me to call my girlfriend back into the Office, which I did and he sincerely apologised to her and said he was only messing about and was very sorry if he'd caused any offence. Paul seemed very sincere and she told him she accepted his apology, he did offer to leave if she wanted him to but we said it was alright, and to be fair within five minutes or so you wouldn't have known anything had taken place only moments before, Paul was very polite, articulate and as he usually was, he was very talkative and entertaining.

At one point Paul looked at me and said I had a right pair of legs on me and had I ever done any training, I told him I'd done Karate for years with Les Carr and that I'd had private lessons since the age of twelve, I'd done weights with Martin Petrauskas since the age of thirteen and I had also gone boxing at Sharlston Colliery with Bob Tuckett for a couple of years from the age of sixteen and this impressed him greatly because he knew the people that I had mentioned very well. Paul told me that my Grandad Dennis was one of the best power lifters he had ever seen and that Dennis had boxed in the Army and he had been a Boxing Champion in his younger days. Dennis used to train every day, even when he was an old man, Dennis had his own gym in Heath House, and was fanatical about this training. Paul told me that his own huge strength came for his legs and that is where he had got his punching power from, to this day I believe he still holds the Deadweight Lifting Prison Record. I believe that Paul was genuinely sorry that day and it was just him trying to test people, which is something he would do, he would just try to see how much he could get away with and push buttons to see how people reacted. He also spoke very highly of his brother in law, and told me he had a book shop on the corner of Wakefield Indoor Market and he really enjoyed going to see him as he would have books for Paul to read, he said he loved going there, and as it happened I gave him a lift up there later that afternoon.

On another occasion, Paul had been walking all round Wakefield Town Centre drunk, causing absolute mayhem walking in the middle of the roads with a bright orange road cone on his head that he had been wearing like a wizard's hat, he had walked down Waldorf Way whilst I had been at the garage with Sean. My Grandad, Dennis, had an MOT Station at the bottom of Waldorf Way and later on in the day I had to take a car down for MOT, when I got there Paul was already sat there in Dennis's Office, "Will you give us a lift Dave lad, if I give you some brass" Paul said, I said "I can't sorry Paul I've only just got here and I've got stuff to do", Paul said "Come on I'll give you some brass" and I said "I'm alright for brass thanks, Paul" and he looked pissed off and said "Well sod yer then". Then Clive Harrison who ran the M.O.T bay for Dennis came up to me a short while later and said "Look, will you give Paul a lift, he'll give you some money for petrol but none of the taxis will take him and no one else will take him either, I've been asking people for ages and nobody will go in the office! Let alone give him a lift!" Clive went on saying it was bad for business and I joked I thought "Paul was the customer complaints representative", but Clive said people were driving off once they had seen Paul and it was causing problems, so he practically begged me to take him into town and give him a lift. I've known Clive most of my life and I would to this day consider him to be a friend, so I went into the Office and said "Alright Paul come on I'll give you a lift" he picked up his traffic cone like it was his most prized possession, and I took him up to his brother-in-law's bookshop as he said he had some books for him, Paul was perfectly fine and polite and gave me a fiver for the petrol and really appreciated the lift, to be fair the state he was in it would have probably been hard for him to walk all that way as he was steaming. He did seem really happy to be going to see his brother in law and he told me he loved going the bookshop to see what books he had, and that his brother in law would put books to one side for him that he had asked for, Paul told me how he adored reading and mentioned several authors, in the end I said look Paul I've got to go as I need to go back down to the garage and get some work done and he went off merrily on his way.

In and around the beginning of the millennium I lived at Peacock and I was studying for my degree in Computers and Paul Sykes was quite often in the local area and quite often on the local buses, although I never catch buses myself. One day my wife had got on the bus with my son, Joseph who was in the push chair and the bus driver had gone to set off as soon as he had taken the money for the ticket, like bus drivers quite often do, regardless of whether it is women with pushchairs or elderly people they just accelerate and people go skittling down the aisle trying not to fall, well on this occasion Paul Sykes was sat at the front of the bus and he jumped up and shouted at the bus driver and made him wait until my wife had sat down and got settled and only then when he had checked that she was ok, did he give the bus driver permission to set off. This happened on several occasions according to my wife and he also used to do the same if old people got on the bus, and to be fair it was a positive thing that people used to comment on, as it is common for people to trip and struggle on and off buses and at times bus drivers can be very inconsiderate to passengers and other road users, so I would see this as a very positive thing that Paul did to assert himself.

I would say about twelve months after that it was well known that Paul Sykes was regularly in Wakefield Bus Station drunk, there were many tales of him causing mayhem and distress to people, in fact I think it featured in the Wakefield Express at the time on many occasions. One particular time, my wife had gone to the bus station, again with Joseph in the pushchair and for whatever reason Joseph was crying and Paul Sykes had gone berserk, shouting "Shut that fucking kid up, before I shut it up" and he was creating and carrying on. Well my wife isn't frightened of people and he had just threatened our son, so she reacted shouting back at him "who did he think he was", "he's just an old drunk" etc etc, and at that point the police came, who at that time were armed with CS Gas and to my wife's amazement they were pussy footing around Paul, asking him to come with them and go somewhere else to sober up, all the time whilst Paul is making threats to shut our Joseph up and my wife responding and all the police did was keep saying to my wife "Please don't provoke him, please don't answer him back", I wasn't there but to be fair it was quite pathetic in my opinion. My wife rang me and I went berserk as he had just threatened my baby boy and she refused to tell me where she was as I had said I would come straight up, so I ended up jumping in the car driving round Wakefield City Centre as I was fuming that he thought it was alright to threaten a baby, especially my son. To be honest I was lucky that I didn't find him that day as I had lost it completely and I could have ended up running him over or anything, as it is just how you react when you are young and hot headed, and I was incensed that Paul Sykes was allowed to stand in the middle of Wakefield City Centre and threaten my little boy.

Paul would often walk around Peacock, Lupset, and Wakefield in a big overcoat and I remember reading in The Wakefield Express that a couple called Maureen and Roy Burnley took Paul in and they found him somewhere to live as he had become homeless, and they wouldn't see him on the streets. I later heard that the flat had been smashed up and wrecked and apparently it had previously been a lovely little flat that they had found for him, I had heard that it was other people that had damaged the flat, although I don't really know if it was Paul or other people who were responsible for the damage. I do know that around this time, when Paul got kicked out of there and ended up back on the streets again, that he was almost always drunk and sleeping rough and really in no fit state at all, and I heard many rumours of people giving Paul a slap or a beating, but to be honest I never really found anyone had any valid bragging rights for beating him at this time in his life, as he really was well passed his best, to be fair the many times I passed him in the car, he had trouble standing and walking never mind fighting anybody. It was around that time I think Paul turned to a Vicar in Wakefield for help, as I remember he needed to go to Specsavers because his glasses were lost or broken but he had an ASBO at that time banning him from the town centre, and he had gone to see a Vicar to explain his plight as he needed his glasses to see, I do believe the Vicar had gone into Court and spoken up for Paul Sykes and he had done everything he could to help Paul, who had been to see him many times and as I remember there was a story about it in the Wakefield Express, if I remember rightly it will have probably been on the front page as anything to do with Paul Sykes usually was!

I last saw my Grandfather I few months before he died, I went to his home to sort his laptop out and before I left he said to me to go and see him anytime for a beer, but I was at college at that point doing my degree and I was skint, I didn't want to go up to see my ultra-successful Grandfather cap in hand so to speak, as so many other people did.

Dennis loved life, he loved his Golf and would play as regularly as he could and he favoured Opera music and Frank Sinatra to listen to mostly, in fact, his funeral song was Frank Sinatra's 'I did it my way'. My Grandfather Dennis was a man with a huge character, he was very successful in life and in business and there are many tales and rumours that have been circulated about Dennis and I have heard many of them, but not many people really know that much about Dennis, and as this is a book about Paul Sykes I think really Dennis's Story is so vast and colourful it really could fill a book of its own!

One of the questions that came up following the First Tuesday "Paul Sykes at Large" Documentary was whether or not Dennis was wearing a wig and the answer is yes, but not just any old wig, Dennis used to go down to London to have his hairpieces custom made and supplied from the same place that Sean Connery and the Royal Family go to, so really they were the best wigs that money could buy. I must admit I can only laugh at the story of Dennis's wig falling off, but I think people should take this with a pinch of salt and in the same genre as Paul's Sykes at Large, in so much as it was probably repeated to you to add a bit of comedy value, I don't believe this really happened. Coincidently Dennis was friends with Clive Harrison who ran his MOT Station and also Clive's partner Glenys, who was a well-known Female Body Builder, her photos used to be in all the gyms in Wakefield, such as Shapers and she really did have a fantastic physique, in fact she is Martin Petrauskas older sister, who I used to train with and Martin himself is a "freak of nature", in a nice way, he is the strongest man I have ever met and he is Sean Bailey's uncle and to be honest Martin was like an Uncle to me when I was growing up from about the age of thirteen when I started weight training with him and going sea fishing with him and his brother Joe Petrauskas. Anyway, Clive and Glenys were abroad with Dennis at one of his properties in Turkey, probably sometime around the mid-nineties, and one morning Glenys said to Dennis "I don't know why you bother with them wigs, you look fine without them, why don't you bin them wigs, you'll look so much better!" and from that day he never wore one of his wigs again.

Sometime before Paul Sykes died in 2006, it could have been anywhere from 2014 onwards my wife ran into Paul at our local shop on Alverthorpe Road, Jacksons, which is a mini-mart type shop, it is now a Sainsbury's Local Store. Well on this occasion Paul Sykes had walked in to the shop after my wife, he had not done anything wrong but the staff immediately started hurling abuse at him, refusing to sell Paul any alcohol, funnily enough Paul wasn't causing any bother that day, he had only just walked into the shop, but the staff took full advantage of the situation telling him nobody was frightened of him anymore, he was a waste of space, he was a has-been etc, and my wife said he was looking very dishevelled and humble, he wasn't abusive, but the staff seemed to take great delight in verbally abusing him, she said he just looked like a broken man. It is fair to say that a lot of people disliked Paul because he had been a bully, but in his last years of life, Wakefield as a whole bullied him, to be fair I am not sure I can make the distinction of why it is alright for people to bully him when he was down, I suppose it is a matter of opinion, but it is not something that impressed me and it just seems sad, and also shows that a lot of people will bully if they can get away with it, Paul Sykes is no exception but the staff at Jacksons, in my opinion, are no better either. Anyway when my wife came out of the shop Paul was sat outside looking and feeling very sorry for himself and my wife asked him if he was ok, she said he was humble and polite, she told him she thought the staff were out of order, and asked if he wanted her to get him some cans, so Paul gave her some money and she went back in, my wife was immediately told that they would not serve her as the cans were for Paul, but despite their reluctance my wife stood up to them and told them Paul might be banned but she certainly wasn't, and if she wanted to buy cans then she would do and despite the difficulties they had to serve her. My wife said Paul was delighted when she came back out of the shop, she gave him his change and he was trying to insist that she took £20 for her trouble as he really appreciated what she had done, she said she had to refuse several times as he was determined to give her the money, she told him that it was fine as long as he was alright and she said he was really very grateful and very polite, she also told him to make sure he put his money away so that nobody tried to take it off him. I don't know if my wife would have got the cans for Paul had she just seen him outside the shop but it was because of the abuse that she witnessed by the staff towards Paul, threatening him, telling him that they would call the police and verbally abusing him, that I think really motivated her to go back in and stand up to them, as bullying, either way, is not really clever, whether people think Paul deserved it or not.

There were other tales that went around about that time about Paul Sykes, they usually featured in the Wakefield Express, on one particular occasion I had heard that Paul Sykes was sleeping rough somewhere near the Peacock Estate and teenagers had poured petrol on him and set fire to him and apparently it had been quite serious, despite whatever he had done when he was younger I cannot see any justification to treat another human being like that, and as a Christian I would say that Paul Sykes spent many years in Prison and he did repay his debt to society, and the people that abused him in his later years are no better than he was in that respect. I have always been aware that Paul Sykes was hassle from the many stories I have heard, he was well known to be able to jump up from being sat down in a millisecond. He was also well known to be fine one minute and then get drunk and then just go berserk without any reason or warning, to cause a lot of mayhem and be out of order, he was well known to get paralytic and get in to fights and to then to come back the next day at 7/8am stone cold sober to finish off what he had started the day before. There are loads of stories like him killing a German Shepherd that had attacked his sister, but from my point of view I am glad for the many times I did see Paul Sykes and speak to him, he could be very articulate and polite and be very insightful, quick witted and amusing, he was entertaining and he really did make you laugh. I appreciate that there is a dark side to Paul Sykes but to be fair I didn't really see that side of him and it is obvious that he had a troubled up bringing living on the Lupset Estate where anybody who has lived or spent any time there will tell you, it really is a case of bully or be bullied. So whilst I am not making excuses for what he has done, I can only call a spade a spade, and from my own experiences of Paul Sykes he was a very intelligent and articulate person and he stood up to people in authority

130

who otherwise would ride roughshod over people, like they do every day of the week, police officers, council employees etc, many of whom are no better, they are bullies, they intimidate people, they abuse their positions of trust and authority and I feel that he did stand up to people, the only difference between him and them is that he was an expert at violence and he rose to a greater status of notoriety.

In all honesty towards the end of his life there was very little positive that I heard, and he did become a public nuisance, it is so sad that he really could have gone further with the boxing if his life had turned out differently, either way, he did make a mark on Wakefield for good or for bad and he was definitely a character, and it was always a unique experience to sit and have a conversation with him.

*    *    *    *

*2nd Interview, carried out after David had read Unfinished Agony*

Obviously, the documentary and Sweet Agony invoke different feelings and emotions now at the age of 41, than they did as a 15-year-old, and reading your book has opened doors to memories that had been locked away, and had me thinking thoughts that I have not thought about for years.

After reading Unfinished Agony I would like to put it on record that I really enjoyed reading your book and I hardly put it down, it was a fantastic read and I particularly enjoyed the different perspectives both good and bad that were experienced by different people who ran into Paul throughout his very colourful life. I would, however, like to put the record straight with a few things, such as, the house that featured in the First Tuesday Documentary is, in fact, Heath House which is a huge Mansion and a very impressive property in the exclusive area of Heath Common, Wakefield.

It has been suggested that Dennis had done a lot of prison, and I can confirm that this is just nonsense, and although local myth and legend may have that down it just isn't true, people used to say the same about my Dad and Mark, that they had criminal records as long as your arm and had done plenty of jail, when in actual fact neither of them have been in prison.

Also, Dennis did move out of Heath House when he sold it in 1999, he then moved on to Rosebarn Cottage, and around that time he did have a girlfriend called Elizabeth but lovingly known to everybody as "Nelson", and yes he was besotted with her but when he sold Heath House and moved into Rosebarn Cottage it was around the same time that Elizabeth was selling her house in Thornes, Wakefield, and she had her own money, she owned her own house and she had owned her own restaurant and she bought an ex-council house on the Eastmoor Estate and Dennis did a lot of work making it into a really beautiful property.

I am also surprised to read comments regarding my Dad, Steven being a bad influence on Paul Sykes because my Dad and Dennis had fallen out and weren't really speaking around the time of the Documentary and anyone who knows my Dad will tell you he didn't need Paul Sykes to sort his problems out or to collect his debts. My Dad has also always been a big bloke and was also well known around Wakefield and like a friend of mine recently described him "he was no shrinking violet", to be honest my Dad was my hero when I was growing up and whilst I think he may have had respect for Paul Sykes, I certainly don't think he was one of his biggest fans.

To be fair it's like other things that have also been said such as people driving passed Heath House and saying "Look, all that was bought by drug money" which again to be brutally honest simply isn't true and I am 110% on my facts that Dennis may have been many things, but one thing for sure is he was staunch anti-drugs, he was from a different generation and he didn't get involved with drugs, he didn't take drugs and he didn't advocate anybody else taking drugs, like I say it is a totally different generation. Make no mistake about it Dennis knew people from all over the Country and he was known all over the Country, he had friends who lived on the Caravan Site at the bottom of Heath Common, friends who lived on Council Estates right through to Multi-Millionaires, MP's and Free Masons, "he got about a bit" but in all honesty he was the right person at the right place at the right time, he took his chances and he made his money, like many people used to say when he was alive "he had the Midas touch".

I think that the First Tuesday Documentary and Paul's Book "Sweet Agony" wet people's appetite and for many years people were waiting for a follow up, and it would appear that there is still a lot of interest out there with regards to people being interested in the life of Paul Sykes otherwise none of your readers would be reading this right now. I have spoken to you (Jamie) and your publishers about the possibility of doing a book about Dennis Flint, and I have been making a start on documenting and researching a book all about his extravagant and very successful life, so watch this space!

If I could say one thing about Paul Sykes it would be that although he may not seem like a role model, I think he could serve as a warning to people that no matter how good you are, drink and drugs really do mess you up, and I think that as human beings we all make mistakes and when you have a high profile these mistakes are seen by more people. Paul Sykes must have been a somebody or people would no longer be talking about him, but if he had steered clear of the drink and the drugs he could have gone so much further, as he had an excitement and a passion for life, along with such huge natural ability, and if he hadn't lost the fight with his own personal demons, I am sure he could have easily gone the distance.

R.I.P. Paul Sykes

*Please note: Contrary to the information received when putting together 'Unfinished Agony', Dennis Flint actually passed away at the age of 68 on the 5th September 2001 whilst resident of Rosebarn Cottage, Heath Common, Wakefield. Please accept our apologies for this inaccuracy.

# WES BOSTOCK

Wes Bostock has just turned 40 years of age and is from Barnsley in South Yorkshire.

In his younger years Wes was in prison quite often. He started off with car crime then this lead on to robberies, armed robberies and then he received a hefty sentence for shooting a man.

Wes has been all over the country in every prison that you can think of. He's not proud of his past by any means and he is now a totally reformed married man who lives the quiet life.

\*     \*     \*     \*

Obviously being a kid from Barnsley, Wakefield is right next door and I live on the Wakefield border, if I got pulled for speeding half a mile up the road I'd be classed as being in West Yorkshire, so I literally grew up three or four streets away from West Yorkshire.

When I was younger, growing up and doing bits of crime I'd hear of all these 'proper faces' so when I was growing up the name Paul Sykes came with a big big reputation of being the number one hard man in Wakefield. If anyone was discussing hard men then his name would always be near to the top of the list in that field.

Many years later when I started going to prison as a young YP the first thing I would get told was "If you go on the cons wing and Sykesy gets hold of you you've had it". I was told so many times that this giant of a man dragged young lads into his cell and 'nonced them' there was all sorts of horror stories that were terrifying to listen to but actually it was a load of bollocks! These stories regarding Paul Sykes never happened trust me.

I went to prison in 1994 and the cult story was if you landed in Armley and Sykesy got a grip of you he was gonna bum ya! Armley was the place I was when I first bumped into Paul Sykes on B Wing in 1999 and within seconds of meeting him I knew all the stories, he was so likeable and approachable towards me I can only speak good of him, regarding the stories I had heard about him.

When I was in there with him in 1999 there was also a big black fella called Hubert Duffus from Chapletown in Leeds and he was always in and out of the nick and well known for being a sex offender. He was well known for knocking his pad mates out, tying them to chairs and raping them, I kid you not and the only man brave enough to share a cell with him, out of all the inmates in there at that time was Paul Sykes.

Duffus had a horrendous previous criminal record for sex offences on men in 1985 and 1993 but Paul didn't give a fuck that he was his pad mate and just took it in his stride for the five months they shared a cell.

He scared the life out of most of the inmates as he was known to just stroll around the prison walking in and out of people's cells, even though he was a sex offender he demanded to be put on a normal wing as he said he could look after himself, he wasn't afraid of anyone and everyone did everything they could to keep out of his way. He was a frighteningly powerful man!

An article in the Yorkshire Post in 2016 about Duffus read:

"A dangerous violent sex offender has been jailed for life for subjecting a man who befriended him to humiliating sexual and physical abuse. Hubert Duffus was told it was likely he may never be released from custody unless he is no longer considered a danger to the public. Duffus subjected his victim to degrading attacks over a two-week period before he was arrested in November last year. Leeds Crown Court heard Duffus had nowhere to live after being released from Prison but befriended the vulnerable victim who allowed him to share his flat in Wortley, Leeds. A jury heard Duffus immediately took over his flat and began to physically and sexually bully the victim. During the trial, the victim described how he was forced to shave off his body hair during the prolonged period of abuse. He also spoke of being 'owned' and being made to sleep on the floor of the flat. Duffus, of no fixed address but formerly of Sholebrook Place, Chapletown was found guilty of rape, attempted rape, assault occasioning Actual Bodily Harm and two offences of sexual assault. He has previous convictions for Sexual and Violent offences dating back to 1985. Duffus was jailed in 1993 for similar serious sexual offences. He also received a six-year sentence in 2007 for the knifepoint robbery of a taxi driver. Judge Rodney Jameson QC said, "During the trial you showed yourself to be a volatile man, if that is not already evident from your convictions, you had a number of explosive losses of temper" the judge added "You simply do not believe anything you have ever done amounts to Sexual Assault you believe what you did was entirely proper and appropriate, self-evidently it is not. You plainly have no remorse". Doctors assessed Duffus as posing a serious risk of causing serious harm to other men in the future and that his behaviour "May never alter". Duffus was told he must serve a minimum of seven and a half years in custody before he can apply for parole but was warned he must go on the Sex Offenders Register for the rest of his life. Detective Chief Inspector Mark Griffin of Leeds District Police said 'Hubert Duffus is a violent man who thought of raping, sexually assaulting and stealing from his victim. The sentence handed down to him is a reflection of the seriousness of his offending and should act as a warning to all others. Duffus now has time inside to consider the consequences of his actions."

Another thing I noticed when I was in Armley with Paul in '99 was that he was always out of his cell. Normally this would be for the Red Bands (prisoners with great trust) or cleaners. Now Paul wasn't a Red Band and he certainly wasn't a cleaner but he was always out of his cell and this was because he'd be on his bell and the screws were that scared of him they'd let him out. Even though Paul at that time would have been 53 they still didn't want any aggro with him. He was still a man with a huge back.

I knew Paul had at times had to live on the streets in '99 but he still kept it together at that time. He wasn't bothered about prison hooch (prison alcohol) he used to say that stuff would make you go blind and that was the reason he was in prison was to keep him off the drink. Being in prison was Paul's time away from the drink and he used to say he could be himself. The only thing Paul was bothered about inside of prison was his pouches of tobacco. The screws would always make sure Paul had his smokes and would often give him some of their own to keep him quiet. Paul Sykes without his smokes would kill a man!

I spent 18 months that time in Armley and the majority of that was with Paul. One story that sticks in my memory of Paul was the time I was on an Anti-Bullying course with him. Paul and I were sat in this classroom and in the afternoon, we got yard time which was to go out and have a walk and a smoke. I was walking around the yard with Paul and a lad from Leeds called 'Coatesy' aka Paul Coates and we're having a discussion and I noticed that this Coatesy had started trying to take the piss out of Paul a bit. I remember Paul saying to him "Where are you going with this Coatesy?" Coatesy looked at Paul and said "Well look at you now you're a wreck of a man, look at me compared to you, I'm like a Ferrari and you're like an old model Volvo" we were still walking whilst this conversation was going on and Paul, like he always did, was walking with his hands behind his back but he calmly stopped in his tracks and said to Coatesy very politely "Listen Coatesy don't start taking the piss, if you're not prepared to fight then you shouldn't argue" this is something that I've told many people over the years and I'll never forget it. Coatesy just kept on and on, outright verbally attacking Paul and trying to belittle him in front of me. Paul then said, "The outcome of an argument is almost always a fight so we'll leave it there". Well Coatesy very foolishly kept going and going until I heard 'BANG' Paul hit him and knocked him spark out, stepped over him and carried on walking with me. I'm talking to Paul and agreeing but at the same time I could see this limp body laid not moving. Paul quietly said to me "But I told him didn't I Wes?" there was nothing else for me to say but "Yes Paul you did".

That was Paul, laying a man clean out on an anti-bullying course break in between classes. A couple of days go by and we're still on this anti-bullying course and we've been asked to do some drama, a kind of role play thing. We were put in groups and given instructions on how to go about things the right way and Paul said, "I want to play the victim".

Paul insisted he had to be the victim and me and a couple of others had to bully Paul Sykes and say nasty things to him as part of this role play, it wasn't the most relaxing situation I've been in I can tell you. We started calling him names and he told us to stop and that we were embarrassing ourselves, he asked us to think of all the horror stories we had heard about him over the years and use them so he meant business! So, the lads that were part of our team start shouting at him and calling a him a nonce and a rapist and that Sykesy fucks YP's and I was like, erm ok lads don't go overboard. Paul thought it was hilarious and was laughing his head off and even joined in, he was shouting "Sykesy is a rapist" that was his dark sense of humour.

I went back to Armley for a different crime around 2002/03 and was to meet up with Sykesy again. I could tell instantly that he was a mere shell of the man he was only three to four years before. By that time Paul couldn't really fight anymore but he was kept safe by his reputation that proceeded him. Guys who didn't know him but knew his name so many of them gave him a wide berth anyway.

After 6 months, I was moved over to E Wing and that's where I came across Paul's son, Paul Junior. I found Paul Sykes Junior to be a bit of a dizzy bastard and he loved the fact his name was Paul Sykes and would relish using his Dads name to people.

I used to tolerate Paul Jnr and was even padded up with him for a short while although he was always sniffing Subutex (prison drug) and he'd be up at 3am shouting out of the windows and I very nearly came to blows with him a few times for it. He did my head in in the end if truth be told.

His older Brother, Michael Sharpe is another who thinks he's like his Dad. I met him in Lindholme and he used to go around bullying people and taking stuff off other prisoners. Michael Sharpe ended up getting beaten up with table legs by a few lads because of his antics. To look at Michael Sharpe you'd think it was a young Paul Sykes as he is identical. It's sad to see because their Dad was a bit of a somebody and they were his sons and the way they are going on well it's embarrassing.

Another of Paul's sons that I've met inside is Adam Sykes. Adam was a bit of a fruitcake when I last saw him, I'm not sure if it was down to the medicine he was on but he was very strange. Adam used to rip bed sheets up and tie apples to them and try to throw them across the landings. I know a few of the lads went to speak to the screws about him saying that Adam wasn't all there and that he needed medical help. The screws would just say "Well he's just a bit odd, look who his father is". I think Adam needed help and shouldn't have been on a normal wing.

Going back to Paul Snr though, when I was with him in 2002/03 in Armley, we'd be lucky to get an hour out of our cells, but Paul wouldn't bother with it, he'd walk in his cell and close the door. I saw a few people gobbing off at Sykesy on a couple of occasions and he didn't want to know, he couldn't be bothered with the hassle. A few years previously he would have eaten them alive, you could just tell he wasn't himself anymore. He just cut himself away from everyone and was happier just talking to the pigeons which he did quite often.

The last time I saw Paul was early in 2007 and I didn't even recognise him, big beard, big coat and he looked the double of Cyril Bruce the famous local tramp in Hemsworth. Cyril Bruce was once a millionaire and gave it all up to live on the streets. Poor Cyril was murdered by a couple of drunks who kicked him to death in a shop doorway and that's exactly who Paul reminded me of when I saw him that day. Paul's face was full of scabs, I don't know whether that was from falling over or being beaten up. He was pissed and I was with my Mrs at the time and I started to tell her the story of who this man once was. She was stunned that day and was almost brought to tears about "That poor man".

I remember being at my Grans house and my Auntie came in and told me that Sykesy was dead. Around Wakefield Sykesy was a bit like Ronnie Kray, that's who he was on a par with in that City. Paul will never be forgotten because when any hard man gets mentioned in Yorkshire, Paul Sykes will never be far from someone's lips.

Paul Sykes went to the University of Life and he was so good at figuring people out. He was a straight ball guy and he didn't take any shit from anyone. He had a soft heart and I'd seen him give away his things to other prisoners who had nothing. If you were a sponger though he would soon suss you out as he had a fabulous intuition about people. In just short of the two years of both sentences that I spent with him I can only speak well of the man. I would go so far to say he was a Gentleman and a true prison legend.

*"I had swum from Singapore to Malaysia and got covered in algae from the water. As I came ashore looking like the jolly green giant I had these thoughts, not in my voice, saying I should return to Britain and write my book. I hope people will get to read me and hopefully like me and when I do the book people will believe me. I have to find an occupation which is legal and which suits my personality. I have a story to tell and this suits me down to the ground. I have never drawn dole money and god did not make me 6ft 3 inches and 16 stone to take orders from bastards"*

**-P Sykes**

# SIMON AMBLER


Simon Ambler is 44 and he grew up in Crofton which is just outside of Wakefield.

I came across Simon through my publishers Warcry Press as Simon's father, Ken Ambler, had written a book that was published on kindle by them. The book is called 'A Coalfield in Chaos' and it's about the miner's strikes that occurred between 1984-1985.

Ken has sadly passed away now but his memoirs of this torrid time are still available via Amazon to purchase for the kindle. Some of the proceeds from this book will be going to The Bradley Lowery Foundation, which is a truly magnificent cause.

Ken was a staunch NUM supporter and throughout all the strike he never broke and was allegedly blacklisted by the government after the strike had finished and because of this he couldn't find work. I'm sure anyone who lived or participated throughout the strike would find this book a very interesting read.

I'd spoken with Simon a few times on Social media and he had told me that he knew Paul Sykes.

*       *       *       *

The first time I ever heard of Paul was around 1985, he was on the news because of his latest imprisonment. I remember his picture came up and the news reader mentioning that he was an ex-boxer from Lupset. I was only 13 at the time but my ears pricked up at his name on the TV because he was local and because a lot of my friends from school would speak about him like he was a local hero. Quite a few kids at school would say "I know Paul Sykes" or "Paul Sykes is my Cousin, I'll get him onto you", they didn't know him and weren't related to him but he was the person to know so the kids often boasted that they knew him. So many boys that were around my age looked up to him, I suppose only because they were young and impressionable.

I wouldn't meet Paul Sykes myself until 2000 when I'd just started work in Cash Converters on Westgate in Wakefield. On this particular day one of my fellow colleagues came running up to me looking very worried, I asked what was wrong and he told me "Paul Sykes has just walked in and I'm not dealing with him" I looked around at the staff we had in that day and apart from me, this guy who wouldn't deal with Paul, a lady who was also too afraid to serve Paul, a young YTS who didn't look too keen and the manager. I had a feeling it would be left to me as I'm 6ft 4 myself and I was right. I took a deep breath and thought 'he can't be that bad really' and walked up to the counter and said, "Yes sir, how can I help you?" He pulled a suitcase onto the counter opened it and said "I've got this to sell", I looked inside and it was full of cheap looking cutlery from China, we saw loads of it and never bought any of it, "I'm sorry Sir we don't buy it" he looked at me with a fixed glare and said "Why not?", I said to him "I'm really sorry, we get loads in and it's just not something we buy, they're just not worth anything, sorry". Paul was with a little lad at the time I think it may have been one of his sons, he just said "Oh ok" packed his things back up into the suitcase and off he went. Now it might have been because he had his young one with him but I like to think that it was how I spoke to him that made him so reasonable that day as the other staff told me after he had left that it was the first time, when he'd been in with a load of tat that they'd refused to buy, that he'd left without a fuss and at the very least telling one of them to "Fuck off".

This happened a little time before things really started to go downhill for him as he was quite well dressed when he came in, he had a suit on, he was a little grey, he never had his beard but he still had his trademark moustache.

A year passed before I came across Paul again. He had been banned by then and he was to keep out of the Town but hadn't stuck to his

ASBO, he was quite obviously drunk and was in the process of being arrested. Naturally there was a bit of crowd stood by watching Paul being put into handcuffs. Someone who was stood watching told me that Paul had just urinated on a young lady, so I thought fair enough, he deserved to be arrested for that but there was an awful lot of police and in my opinion, they were being overly aggressive with him when there was no need to be, he wasn't going anywhere or putting up a fight. I went over to the police officers and said to them "I can see what you're doing to him and there's no need for it, he's still a human being". My case for standing up for Paul quickly evaporated when he turned around and spat on one of the female police officers, he was quite rightly then marched away. In my opinion, he would have had a case for police brutality in broad daylight with many witness' before that but spitting on a police officer was indefensible in my book.

When I saw him again it was at the side of Wakefield Prison, there's a lane called Balne Lane where the library was and Paul used to hang around outside there. I was about to go inside the library when I noticed Paul sat there on a mat of cardboard, this was around 2003 and his decline was clearly visible even from the last time I had seen him only a few years earlier. He didn't seem drunk and he looked up at me and said, "Ere big lad come and sit down" and he offered me some of his pork pie. He told me that he had remembered me from Cash Converters and I think he just wanted some company and someone to talk to. I sat with Paul and he started telling me all about his life and some of the things he had done. How he ran 'Threaten-a-grams', swam with crocodiles, fought with the Mafia and he told me how he used to travel the UK selling his fake jewellery. One of the things he did tell me that did make me laugh was when he warned me to keep away from the boxing promoter Don King, like there was a chance that I would ever come across him! Paul warned me to stay away from him, he described him as "A horrible man". Paul told me that King had done him wrong many years ago during his boxing career at a time when Paul had trusted him, he also said he did other work for King outside of boxing and Paul's words were "He had me over big time".

I was talking to Paul for what must have been a good half an hour, it honestly felt like only five minutes though because he was such an interesting person to talk to and to listen to. I told him that he used to train with my Dad as kids at the White Rose Boxing Club and he remembered my Dad. I could have stayed there all day talking to him!

He kept trying to offer me some of his pork pie, I asked him where he had got it from he said, "Someone give it me", he said he hadn't eaten anything other than that pork pie since the day before and here he was kindly offering to halve it with me. I wanted to give him some money but I knew only too well what he would spend it on if I gave him cash so I went across to the shop instead and bought him a sandwich and a soft drink. Paul was made up, he was so grateful and repeatedly thanked me for buying him some dinner. I said goodbye to Paul, he wished me well and I left him to it.

I could sense that he was a genuine man with strong morals. I knew he was getting treat badly by people on a daily basis and it was making his life more difficult that it already was.

When Paul died it made Calendar News, he was very well known for one thing or another.

I know people have different opinions about him, but I enjoyed speaking with him that day even if it was only for a short time.

# RICKY WRIGHT-COLQUHOUN

Ricky Wright-Colquhoun is 42 and from Pontefract but now lives in Sheffield.

Ricky approached me via the Sykes – Unfinished Agony Facebook page. He had sent me an inbox and unfortunately it had gone in to the 'other messages' folder and I only found it three months after he had sent it, but better late than never. I am really grateful though that I came across it eventually as Ricky had some great insight as to who Paul was.

Ricky messaged me as he'd just finished reading Sykes-Unfinished Agony and although he really enjoyed it and said it was a brilliant read it left him with a sense of sadness as he'd read Sweet Agony many years before when he was an amateur boxer at the age of 12 and over the years that followed Ricky had the chance to get to know Paul Sykes as Ricky worked in Wakefield and would often pass Paul and spend some time with him.

As a Mental Health Support Worker Ricky told me that if Paul Sykes was alive today that he would have been sectioned over and over again as his violence was likely to be a personality disorder associated with alcohol abuse. He also said that even watching the Paul Sykes at Large documentary, as he had many times, that although Paul was very intellectual he was always grandiose in this perception of himself.

*     *     *     *

My first recollections of the name Paul Sykes was as a naïve young boy at the age of 10 in 1985. I remember it clearly. I had always been interested in boxing since watching my first fight on television. This happened to be Barry McGuigan defeating Eusebio Pedroza. From that night a fuse was lit, I was completely hooked and Instead of the Beano and Smash-hits, that other peers my age were reading, I started reading the old black and white version of Boxing News. In those days, it was a newspaper.

The first edition I got had an article in it about this very interesting fighter by the name of Paul Sykes. It was reviewing his British title fight with John L Gardner. This was a fight in which he had lost by stoppage in the 6th round. By the time I came to read this review Paul was back in prison and by all accounts his life was unravelling.

I don't know what it was but I was intrigued by this character, a ruffian who was constantly in trouble with the Police, yet somehow had a strange tinge of mystique about him.

All my school friends who were all boxers kept talking about this new book. It was called Sweet Agony originally released in 1990. This book was about Paul Sykes, the very man I had read about in the early paper edition of Boxing News. I bought the book and from the moment I started it, I couldn't put it down. It was almost like a caricature of this man that bullied and frightened people, turned up in the dark and if you were unlucky enough to have upset him you were likely to get a clump.

On the other hand, something about him appeared to be likeable, his sense of humour came across in the book. I read this book repeatedly and concluded that he was misunderstood by the authorities and that the book had been slightly fabricated by Paul Sykes to make the book more interesting.

By the year 2000 I was working in Wakefield and at the same time was training for my professional boxing licence. I was training out of Normanton social club near Wakefield. It was during this time that I got to know Paul Sykes, the real person.

The first time I saw him was in Wakefield bus station. He had blue dungarees on and a large florescent donkey jacket. To be frank he looked like a giant, he had massive hands and he was as broad as he was tall. This was only 10 'o' clock in the morning yet he was cradling a can of special brew and growling. People in the bus station ignored him. For the local people, this was obviously a common sight for them.

That first time I saw him, although I wanted to speak to him he had quite an intimidating presence so I walked on by.

Over the coming months I would keep on seeing him and the local people would tell me that Paul had chronic arthritis and was to all intents and purposes homeless and sleeping in the grave yard, among other places.

The second time I saw him was in the market place in Wakefield and to be honest I felt sorry for him. He was trying to open a can of special brew, which he couldn't do because his hands were so damaged from boxing. I witnessed quite a sweet moment, a little old lady walked over to him and opened it for him, she sat down and spoke to Paul and he chatted away quite happily with her for 10 minutes. I was shocked that he was that approachable.

I went over to him and sat down with him, I explained that I was training to be a boxer and his eyes lit up immediately. You could tell instantaneously that boxing was something he loved. There was a burger van next to us and I asked him if he wanted a burger as it didn't look as though he had a regular meal in some time to me. I bought him a burger and started to speak to Paul, I said "I watched your fight with John L Gardner on video" and it was then that Paul became really animated about the fight and he could still remember every round as though it was yesterday. As he was talking he would be throwing miniature shots to mimic the type of shots he liked.

I kept bumping into him over the next couple of months, and was quite surprised when he recognised me but he did and he would always ask how the training was going as he knew my trainer quite well.

I would see him on many occasions walking down the street in a really dishevelled manner, sometimes urinating against the wall and constantly talking to himself. This was obviously a shadow of the former man that the book Sweet Agony portrayed.

To many of the people in Wakefield he was a folk hero, unless perhaps they had been on the receiving end of a right hander. Everybody knew him and had tales to tell whether good or bad.

My own memories of Paul are feeling sorry for him. He would often show up with bruises from another beating by young teenagers that wanted a name for themselves.

In the end, he really needed support but that came much too late. He was skin and bone and the last time I saw him he had a huge bushy beard that was greyed and several layers of clothes on. His eyes were jaundice and his skin pallid.

I went over to him and said hello, I was saddened that he didn't know who I was on the last time I spoke to him but I gave him a fiver and went on my way.

I followed his progress over the next couple of years and he just unravelled and went from one unfortunate encounter to another. I must admit when I heard that he had been found unconsciousness near a bus shelter and a few days later had passed away, I felt some dignity for him had been restored and at last he had some peace.

Rest well Paul, a Yorkshire giant.

# TRACEY THOMPSON

Paul Sykes lived in a man's world, he was his own boss and lived by his own set of rules.

Predominately most of the interviewee's I've spoken to whilst researching for both books have been male, so I'm always grateful when a woman gets in touch to say that she knew Paul Sykes, the one off from Lupset. After all, each of the people in these books have a tale to tell and for me it is just paint that keeps adding to the picture of who Paul was. Not every interview made the books but although brief, I wanted to add Tracey's account and I felt there was a powerful message behind it.

\*     \*     \*     \*

I'm from Wakefield and I'm 55 years old. Around 2001 I was the Security Manager for Asda in Durkar, Wakefield for a time. Before I started the job, I was briefed about this big troublesome figure by the name of Paul Sykes. Most of my colleagues would say he was an ex-boxer turned 'wrong un'. I was told about all the encounters the previous Security Manager had had with this man and that he was normally very loud and aggressive, reportedly the only trouble the store ever had was when Paul would go in every few weeks, bringing all hell with him for as long as he was in the store.

After a few weeks of being in the job hearing about this urban legend, the time had come for me to meet this much talked about character in the flesh. A couple of work colleagues were running around frantically looking for me to inform me that Paul Sykes was in the Cafeteria and he was shouting, causing a bit of a scene and carrying on. I went to the café and saw him sat there, customers were stood around gawking at him like they would if someone had collapsed in the market! "Are you alright Paul?" I asked him in a very un-confrontational manner. I could tell by his body language that I'd totally thrown him by talking to him in warm friendly way. He thought I'd gone over to throw him out which wasn't the case at all. I sat and spoke with him and listened to him and I noticed this calmed him down considerably. I think we just had idle chat about the weather and the little things in life. He was aware of the large crowd that had gathered around him staring which was making him edgy but when I spoke to him and showed him some understanding and compassion he really calmed down, his whole demeanour changed.

I knew that day that if I'd used the wrong approach with Paul it would have been the trigger for him to really go off it. I was aware of his history and his 'bad lad' reputation but because I didn't judge him and I gave him the time of day he was completely different to all the tales I'd heard of him. I kept eye contact and showed him some warmth and he was fine.

My opinion of him that day was that he was a lost soul, in pain mentally and it was sad to see a man like that. I 'd heard so much about how he'd been a somebody once upon a time but he looked nothing but a shell of the menace that I'd been expecting to meet.

After speaking to Paul for maybe 10-12 minutes he stood up, said thanks and goodbye and went on his way peacefully and without any trouble. I felt that I'd handled the situation the right way, I'm sure if I'd have marched up to him and ordered him out things would have gone very differently but my take on him was that actually he was probably mentally ill and he had real issues.

He was used to people judging him and him having to take the world on alone, I didn't want him to feel like that that day, if only more people had taken the time to listen to Paul I think he may have behaved differently at times, it's all very sad.

# ANDY HAMMOND

Andy Hammond is 50 years old this year and born and bred in Wakefield, in Eastmoor to be precise. Andy has his own business and puts solid roofs on conservatories.

He came across the Paul Sykes site on Facebook and messaged me through that and told me about his experiences of Paul, I was delighted that he agreed to be interviewed for this book.

*     *     *     *

The first time I heard the name Paul Sykes I was only very young, just a lad really and my friend's father Harry Curry used to work on the door of the Mecca, unfortunately Harry passed away a few years ago but Harry used to tell us all stories about Sykesy being a pain in the arse to him and every doorman in the town.

It wasn't only Harry that I heard this from as I had family on the Lupset estate who all knew Paul very well. Everyone and their dog knew what he was like and often peoples overall opinion about Paul was that "He was alright when he was sober but when he'd had a drink he'd start a fight with anyone" that is what the majority thought about him. When I say alright I mean as normal as Sykesy got, everyone was very aware of his presence when he was around. It would be probably fair to say that I don't think he set out to cause havoc, when he was sober he was a very quiet guy, but it just happened that havoc was exactly what he caused the more drink he had in him. Only when he had a drink in him did he become lairy and it was almost like he felt he had to prove himself as he'd built up a hell of a reputation for himself as a lad and when he went into prison his reputation snowballed and I think he always played up to that.

My Step-father was a prison guard in Wakefield and New Hall and he even said that Paul preferred to be in prison then out, it was the only place he could just be himself. He had no alcohol problems or distractions while he was locked up and even Paul used to say he was more at ease with himself while he was behind bars. My Step-father grew up on the Lupset estate so he knew Sykesy on the outside and while he was in Prison so I think he was more than qualified to comment on the differences that Paul exhibited during his stints of freedom and incarceration.

Paul was great friends with a huge family from the Lupset estate called the Riley family. They were pretty much cut from the same cloth as Paul and it was easy to see why he got on with them but they all mellowed with age whereas Paul didn't.

I'd say the time I had the most to do with Paul was between 2002-2007 when he was really down on his luck and as much as he'd done in his past, I just felt so sorry for the guy I felt he needed a break! I'd seen him being a bastard to people with my own eyes, I'd heard the terrible tales from people with my own ears but when you're in the shit state he was in, someone offering you a bite to eat or a brew must have been a godsend. There were many times that I stopped in the centre of town to buy Paul a brew.

I'm not under any illusions, the Paul Sykes from 2002-2007 was still a nasty bastard but the threat of violence from him had gone. He was often seen in the precinct growling at people walking by or if he had more of his wits about him that day he would be shouting at them. People would shout back at him telling him "Get a grip Paul you're living on the streets", but most would just ignore him. Paul would often be seen just sat staring into space or talking to the pigeons and 80% of the time he was unapproachable unless you were offering him something that is. He would tap cigarettes from kids and his appearance was awful, you could tell the drink had already killed the man before he died. I'd had first-hand experience of watching someone drink themselves to death, my Mum's sister, my Auntie, had done just that and she was only 31, I recognised the signs and I'd look at Paul around 2005/06 and think to myself that it wouldn't be long before he was a fucking goner, that he didn't have long left and unfortunately, I was right. You only had to look at him, he was bruising easily and a lot of his blood vessels had come to the surface of his skin. Just the way he walked made you visualise the damage he was doing to his organs. Around 2005 it started to affect him very badly, he was just waiting to die by then.

I used to shout to him "Paul do you want a brew?" he'd always say, "I'd love a cup of tea kidda" he was always very gracious If you offered him anything, if he knew you were trying to help him he would always be grateful to you.

Around 2006 I used to be friends with people who worked down the boat yard on Don's Lane, I used to take all my pallets there from work for the boss to burn on the bonfire. When I went down there I found out that Paul was living in the yard as he could sleep on the Sofa's so he'd be safer and a bit warmer on a night. This was just after Paul had been set on fire by kids with lighter fluid. Some of those youths used to piss on him when he was asleep.

The owner of this yard, a fella called Bruce had heard what had happened and took him to live in his yard away from the kids that hunted him in their packs. Paul knew that Bruce was trying to save his life and he was really grateful to him for that, even though he was still sleeping outside the bonfire would be blazing all night so it kept him warm.

I would often see Paul on the precinct or at the top of Westgate stumbling around, I would nip to Greggs for him sometimes and get him a pasty, sausage roll and a cuppa and I'd go over and sit with him for 10 minutes to listen to what he had to say. He never used to make much sense by then though and truth be told I could never understand him very well, I just used to nod and shake my head and pretend I understood every word then I'd be on my way, at least he'd had a feed I used to think.

Paul had just given up on life. The police used to arrest him just to give him a wash and clean him up then they would let him go again.

Obviously, the police would get a lot of complaints about Paul, not only just about his behaviour but he'd become a bit of a Health and Safety issue really! I don't mean to sound awful but I took him a cup of tea one day, Paul stood up to get it and shit himself there was literally shit falling out of his trousers!

I always thought it was a shame to see Paul like that but it was as if he wasn't house trained. If they'd have put him in sheltered accommodation he was such a cranky bastard that it wouldn't have lasted long so I don't think there were many other alternatives in Paul's case. He was a nasty drunk and that was a fact, he couldn't leave the drink alone and that about sums up all his problems in life.

Paul was a waste of talent and I remember watching him box on telly and I've also read his book Sweet Agony that he wrote while he was in prison and I know from that alone that he was an intelligent guy. He was on the wrong tracks from day one and I'm sorry to say that those were the tracks he stayed on his whole life as much as he might have tried to be something different, it was all he knew. Paul had plenty of opportunities to lead a better life, he wasn't thick was he but he chose the way he went and that was that. It's very sad but true. Someone with his intellect could have been a fantastic full-time author he could have done almost anything that he wanted to but we'll never know his capabilities now will we.

I don't understand why some people from Wakefield have the view that they don't even want to mention his name, even on some of the Facebook groups, he's dead, it's not like he's going to harm anyone anymore.

Paul Sykes might have been a complete nob at times when he was alive but karma caught up with him and then some more for good measure. The end to his life wasn't very nice believe me I saw him.

The people that were cruel to him at the end of his days had fuck all reason to be cruel to him, he never hurt those kids. Paul was too weak and frail to hurt anyone at that time regardless. Those youths just wanted to make a name for themselves by hurting someone with the reputation that Sykesy had, just to say that they had beat him. It was terrible what happened to that man. I remember seeing him after a gang of youths had set fire to him, was there any fucking need I thought. I had an idea who it was, well should I say I'd heard a story, and if it is to be believed, they didn't fucking know him from Adam really, they had no reason at all apart from them trying to get bragging rights by saying that they'd sorted Sykes out. I was just hoping that the bastards got caught for it and sent down for it but they never caught anyone. Absolute scum of the earth, you don't set someone on fire! Some young lads would walk past him in the street and give him a crack in the face for nothing, he was just a vulnerable man at this point and totally incapable of defending himself anymore.

Paul Sykes had a ferocious name for himself but that's all it was, it was a one-way situation I'm afraid and poor Paul copped a few beatings. He was never sober anymore, even if he hadn't had a drink that morning he was still always drunk from the night before, he just didn't give a shit about anything in life anymore.

I'm not sure if you're aware but if you're an alcoholic the beer feeds you and you don't eat, so nothing stays there so if you've had a drink there's nothing to keep it in and that was the reason that Paul was always shitting himself my poor Auntie was the same god bless her.

We should be talking about Paul Sykes the award-winning author or the British Heavyweight Champion at the very least.

Paul Sykes is still very much spoken about in Wakefield to this day. People in Lupset will remember him as a bully, but he wasn't a bully with everyone in Wakefield and that's why there's so many mixed feelings about Paul even to this day.

When Paul Sykes died we all knew it was coming but it was very much the talk of the whole town that's for sure. Paul was a larger than life character and he'll be remembered probably more than anyone else from Wakefield from his era. I knew a few bad lads like Dennis Flint, Tony Williams, Paul Burke and Ernie Fields but they'll never be remembered like Paul Sykes is.

Dennis lived off the names of people who looked after him because he had a lot of money.

At the end of the day Paul Sykes was a human being he fucked up his life and he knew it at the end because he told me one day having a cup of tea. He had committed many crimes and he served his time for them.

Paul's only friends were people on the wrong side of the law and he'd do people favours but it would be things like getting money debts from people who owed his mates that sort of thing.

Paul Sykes' legendary reputation went before him and he was always news worthy most weeks in the Wakefield Express and I'm sure they used to think that if they had fuck all else to write about that week that they'd just stick Paul in.

Most of us will live and die and not be remembered in 50 years' time like he will be. That in itself is an achievement, isn't it? Paul Sykes made his mark in the world as crazy as it sounds and fucking good on him!

# SHAUN HIRST

Shaun Hirst is from Normanton and is now 32 years of age. In 2001 he was a young man with fake ID.

It's all very well putting your former Boxers, Prisoners and Bouncers in the book with their views on Paul Sykes but I was interested in getting a slightly different perspective and I think Shaun's interview provided that.

*　　*　　*　　*

I was 17 years of age in 2001 and I'd managed to get myself into The Terrace nightclub with the help of some fake ID, it was in there that I heard about Paul Sykes.

I'd always been into the combat sports myself such as Boxing and Wrestling and I've always been drawn to the biggest and baddest in them sort of sports so that day when I overheard a crowd of burly men covered in tattoos talking about this guy they called 'Sykesy' it was that that raised my initial interest. The way they spoke about him it was like he was on another level to the gents that I was sat with. I've always had an interest in people who were a bit extreme or considered 'different' so I just sat in awe whilst listening to all these stories of this 'Sykesy'.

They spoke of other incidents that had gone on but then came the "It wouldn't have happened if Sykesy was there" or "It wouldn't be like that if Sykesy walked in", I suppose very much like East Enders would talk about the Kray Twins now, you know how people would say that things wouldn't have happened if Ron and Reg were still about, it was the same sort of thing with this Paul Sykes fella that I was hearing about.

So, from that day my thoughts were "Who the hell was this man?" the fact that guys that I looked up to as a young man were talking so highly about this Paul Sykes made me even more curious so when I got home the first thing I did was ask my Dad about him his reply was "Yeah yeah Son I've heard of him but don't you be looking up to him, he was notorious in the 1960's/70's etc".

He told me that Paul was a championship level boxer of course that only intrigued me even more, I couldn't believe he was a boxer as well! It made sense now why these hard cases from the club had all been talking about him like they were in awe of him too.

Your professional athlete will always beat your backyard brawlers which is what those guys essentially were. This guy that I'd already become obsessed with learning about was a skilled guy. So, what the fuck had happened to him was what was forefront of my mind now. My Dad didn't know and others that I'd asked from Normanton didn't know either. There was no Google back in 2001 but I continued trying to find out as much as I could about this man.

Many months later, it must have been about February in 2002 I was at Shooters Bar in Wakefield and it was the end of the night, I remember being sat down on my own when these two men, who were both about 10 years older than me came over and sat close by, we started chatting, you know how it is when you're drunk and you speak to anyone. So, I just came out with it and asked them both if they'd ever heard of Paul Sykes. They both looked at me a bit funny and I was starting to feel a bit uncomfortable like maybe I'd said the wrong thing, when one of them said to me "He is fucked", I'll never forget that. I was sat thinking "Well wow the plot thickens" so I asked, "What do you mean what happened to him?" they went on to tell me how he was a tramp and an alcoholic now. I was so shocked to hear that after all my research that this guy who was spoken about in clubs like someone godlike and who was a professional boxer was being spoken about like this!

I decided to ask a few more questions while I had the opportunity like, "Where does he live" and "What does he do?" They said, "You can see him in the town centre lad, really big scruffy guy walking around" that wasn't precise enough for me so I asked, "Yeah but where abouts, how will I know its him?" "Trust me Son as soon as you see him you'll know" so I left it at that.

The very next week I saw him with my own two eyes and I'd see him for the next five years at it would happen as I was going to college in Wakefield.

That first time I saw him he was outside McDonalds. This is where I used to see him the most but I remembered those two guys saying to me "You'll know him when you see him" and they were right. He was laid up against a pillar holding a can, there were about five or six people stood around him, they looked scruffy too and I'm almost certain they were druggies. Paul sat in the middle of them like he was their leader, his voice was booming so it sounded like he was shouting rather than talking, he was so loud he'd have been perfect as a monster in a big movie with his deep troll like voice. I'd often hear him before I saw him.

That first time I saw him, even though he'd declined greatly by that time he was still twice the size of anyone near him. He was sat there in his black leather jacket with many layers on underneath and this only added to his immense size. It was all very bizarre, here was this man that I'd been so eager to find out about so eager to see and I didn't know what to make of it all. I spent quite a time just watching him thinking "So you're the former boxer that all the fuss was about, it was you that had the reputation", I couldn't quite believe that the down and out that I was looking at was spoken about like he was, all the tales I'd heard. I don't mind admitting that I'd often walk the long way to or from college to see him and even if I didn't see him I would know he was about because you'd hear him!

What I did notice about Paul was his response to people who would say hello to him, it didn't matter if they were Male or Female his response would be the same "Hello flower" he'd say.

I'd see Paul in town and I'd learn quite a bit more about him but I didn't speak to him until the Summer of 2002, that was in a takeaway. I'd ordered a pizza and I was sat waiting for it when low and behold

I look up and there was this imposing figure in the door way. I was aware that he wouldn't be the threat that he had once been but it was his unpredictability that had me worried if I'm honest, the not knowing if something was going to kick off or not. He certainly had an energy coming from him and I didn't know what to think. He came over to me and put a massive hand on my hand and said "Ey up lad"! His hands were without doubt the biggest hands I've ever seen. He hadn't moved his hand when he said to me "What pizza ya getting lad?" I told him I was getting a margarita "I like them can I have some?" he said, I told him of course he could it hadn't been served yet, they were still making it "You used to be a boxer, didn't you?" I asked him and when I said that his whole face lit up and he smiled, he only had a few teeth left and most of them were stumps.

Paul started reeling off all the different sparring partners he'd had, he sat and told me about how he used to spar with Ernie Fields. Listening to Paul I found him to be very pleasant, friendly with a great sense of humour. My pizza came and I sat sharing it with Paul, I felt quite at ease not threatened like I thought I might.

As time passed I noticed that a few of my mates who I'd been out with were coming in to the takeaway but they'd seen that I was with Paul and kept their distance. When they'd collected their food one of them came over to tell me that they were leaving. Paul asked me if this guy was my friend and when I told him it was Paul told me that he didn't like him and that he had "Rubber lips". I'm sure Paul was just messing about and he hadn't meant anything malicious by it. My friends left then shortly after, three rowdy lads came in and Paul started hurling abuse at them. Paul with his megaphone voice started effing and blinding at these three blokes so they in turn started on him calling him a tramp and other words to that effect. Paul arose from where he'd been seated with me, he was very groggy and obviously still very drunk but he faced these three lads and said "Right, step outside gentlemen". I stayed inside but Paul went out followed by the three lads, within seconds of him getting outside he had adopted his boxing stance and was ready, at this moment a couple were walking from the precinct and got in-between it all, I think one of them must have given the lads a heads up because they said that someone had told them "That's Paul Sykes haven't you heard of him you don't want to be fighting with him". You could tell that something had been said without being told because these lads weren't the same confrontational lads that they'd been 15 minutes earlier. They walked away from Paul very quietly and left him in his boxing stance rocking back and forth.

Weeks later I would see Paul again at The Clarence Park Festival in Thornes Park. It was a boiling hot day and Paul was just laid out on the grass on his own minding his own business his head propped up by a cider bottle as a pillow. He didn't cause any bother but I was aware of the dozens of people talking about him saying "Oh look it's Paul Sykes" he seemed oblivious though.

Another occasion when I spoke to Paul was when I saw him on the steps of the old indoor market which is now Trinity Walk, I approached him this time and said "Ey up Paul do you remember me?" he just started laughing with his can in his hand, he didn't really answer me he was just in a drunken haze laughing away to himself, I'm not even sure he knew what was going on he just said, "Ere kid I've got rabies and all sorts" then just burst out laughing some more.

From the first time I saw Paul, I would say that he looked every bit the hobo that was sleeping rough, that never changed until the last time that I saw him. The only change I saw in him was with his walking. By 2005 he was almost crippled compared to even the year earlier I'd say.

One of the last times I ever saw Paul was in the Summer of 2006 and it was the saddest. I didn't know it then but it would have a big effect on my life for many years to come. I was walking through town onto a path and I could hear someone who sounded like they were in absolute agony "Arrrggghhh arrrghhh", loud and painful grunting noises, I wasn't sure where it was coming from until I turned around and saw Paul on the floor writhing about in utter pain, if I was to describe the scene I'd say it looked like Paul was fighting something, like he was actually fighting for his life but there was nothing there. It was baking hot in the sun and he still had all those layers on, Paul started to grasp at invisible things that were in the air, like he was trying to catch something, he was screaming obscenities "Get off me, fuck off and leave me alone" I didn't know what was going on with him, I walked off and left him to it as I just didn't know what the hell was wrong with him, I know differently now but back then I just thought it was Paul just being Paul.

Years later I had major issues with alcohol myself on a pretty bad scale. I had to go into a rehab centre and on to a detox programme. I drank that much that I got DT's and that is when I started to hallucinate and see things. This is the point, it's quite significant that I was telling you about Paul trying to grab at mid-air that day I saw him, as I went through it, I only realised what was happening to Paul that sunny day when I went through it myself in 2013. It made me really upset because I'd never heard of the DT's in 2006 I had no clue at all when I saw Paul not until my own alcohol related breakdown. If I'd have known then what I know now I'd have ran and got him a beer, it was the worst thing I'd ever experienced in my life by quite a mile. I had such a horrific time with hallucinations, brain zaps, extreme anxiety and really bad shakes. I'd describe it as hellish and I had it nowhere near as bad as it looked like Paul had that day. When I had the DT's I was in bed, clinging to dear life, I'd hallucinate about seeing rats scurrying around bee's and butterflies in the air, I felt like I was at deaths door quite literally but I had the support of friends and family, I wasn't alone with no one to help me like he was I think back and think about that poor man laid in the mud, homeless with nothing and no one. He didn't have people feeding him Vitamin B tablets or lifts to the hospital like I had. Still, he was fighting back at whatever it was that was trying to get him that day lashing out at thin air at the things flying above his head. I can't stress enough how much of a damn tough guy he was, I honestly mean that and I don't say that to glorify him either, that's from the heart. It made me realise Paul had spirit, he wasn't laying down he was fighting.

Not only did Paul have to battle DT's he also was regularly attacked by gangs of young people, it's unthinkable and I don't even know what to say about the matter other than feel sorry for that poor poor man. By the end of that man's life he had gone through every barrier that's physically possible, his later life was just hardcore in every way that you could imagine.

The very last time I ever saw Paul was at the bottom of Westgate, he was laid comatose with his head resting on a cider bottle like I'd seen him before in the park and he was with a woman who must have been in her 40's I'd say. Towards the end of 2006 I'd only ever see him with this woman, he no longer had the entourage of followers he'd had about five years previously. I'd been walking down from a night out trying to get a taxi and I could see Paul on the floor. The first thought I had, to tell you the truth, was "How the fuck are you still alive" he had destroyed himself.

I was with a mate of mine and we saw three young lads about 16/17 years old and they were all kicking him, this was about 3am in the morning. My mate and I chased these lads away and they ran off, the woman that was with Paul was shouting at them "You wouldn't have done that 10/15 years ago". I looked at Paul and he was totally unaware of what was even going on. That was the last time I ever saw him alive.

Paul Sykes is a Wakefield legend for all the wrong reasons, it seemed to me like he didn't have a grasp on his emotions.

I believe that Paul attacked a lot of people out of fear because he had been hurt so much in life. Happy people that are content in life just don't need to do that to other human beings, they have no compulsion to do that.

I think a lot comes from his youth and being frightened to death as a child, that along with a personality disorder just made him into this one-off character that Wakefield will probably never see the likes of again.

Many months later in March 2007 I read the news in the Wakefield Express that Paul had died. This really saddened me even though I wasn't his best friend or anything but for the last few years I would see this man almost daily then he was gone, just vanished. It was strange not to hear that voice anymore and even though I knew he was dead automatically in my head I would be looking for him when I went into town.

Paul's death was the end of an era for the whole of Wakefield if you like. Everyone knew him or had heard of him and he's still very much spoken about today.

Throughout the years I've heard a wide spectrum of tales about Paul Sykes ranging from people being angry and disgusted by him to people having a lot of admiration and respect for him. However, for me I can only report back on how I found him from my own experiences.

# JANET

Surname withheld by request

Janet is from Wakefield and is a mature woman. I met Janet in Northallerton at a charity function that I had organised which was "An evening with John L Gardner".

Janet is a born again Christian and spends her entire life helping people less fortunate than herself, very much like my friend Gram Seed.

Janet graciously agreed to speak with me and we met for a chat in a lovely little old pub called The Fleece in Northallerton.

\*       \*       \*       \*

I first heard of Paul Sykes in the late 1970's when I was a teenager. I heard he was a boxer, that some said he wasn't a very nice person and his name was always notorious even though I'd never met him.

From what I had heard about Paul I didn't like him. I knew even though I'd not met him that he was a very angry man from the stories that I had heard on the Wakefield grapevine. I never thought I would have ended up giving Paul Sykes the time of day let alone allow him to move into my home!

I actually met Paul's son Jacob before I met Paul as I worked as a teaching assistant at the same school Jacob went to, sometimes I would look after Jacob as well. There was a lot of talk about him being Paul Sykes' son in the school but I found Jacob to be a little darling, he was a lovely boy, he could be a little swine of course, they all can but I loved him he was lovely for me usually.

I'll tell you how I met Jacob's Dad. I used to be in an abusive marriage,

I was for many years and it led me to have a mental breakdown. I was put in Field Head Mental Hospital (used to be Stanley Royd) in Wakefield in April 2001 and this is where I first met Paul Sykes. Paul was in there trying to keep himself off the booze and he was on medication to help him detox, I can't remember the name of the medication but he was on Valium as well. I clearly remember thinking, before I had even spoken to him that he had an aura about him, he gave off vibes that he was the 'big I am'. He was looking very dishevelled, like he needed a shave and kind of mucky looking but it was nothing to the extent of how he would end up looking just a few years later.

Paul used to wear this big black leather jacket and he used to walk about the hospital with this air of domination about him. This was probably the reason that I didn't speak to Paul for about the first ten days whilst we were in that hospital together. It seemed to me that he had this barrier up anyway, there was a sense that he wasn't so much untouchable but more of a sense of 'come and speak to me if you dare' coming from him in abundance. I ignored it anyway and I did go up and speak to him.

I must have been in his company about two weeks and I told him that I knew his Son, he looked at me and asked me which one and when I told him it was Jacob, it was like the ice had been broken and that we had been best friends for years. He wanted to know all about the school he went to, he wanted to know everything I could tell him.

We spoke about all his family that day. He spoke about Paul Junior and he had so much pride for his kids but also a lot of pain too. Paul told me he could see some of them were going down the same path as him but I think he was torn as he also had a bit of pride that his kids were so strong and took no crap from anyone but he told me he didn't want them to follow in his footsteps.

Paul used to talk about how he felt he'd been a massive failure as a father but that he thought he had this huge reputation to uphold too. He said he had such a strong sense that he should keep up with his reputation even if it meant life or death because it was such a big part of who he was, that it pained him to keep it up but that he felt incapable of stopping it but he did struggle with it.

We were in each other's company daily and spent so much time talking. From that first day onwards, we got on extremely well and I used to sit and listen to him and I think he used to love that.

Paul was doing so well keeping away from the drink but one day we went for a walk with a couple of others, we walked into town and Paul went into a shop and undid all his good work by buying cans of Special Brew. One of the others that was with us, a bald guy called Mark bought some because Paul had bought some and told me he had been told to get some. I was really angry with the pair of them, I was absolutely furious with them and I wasn't scared of Paul, which surprised me but I really wasn't, I implored him not to drink them and I told him he was stupid and walked away from the group. Paul ignored my pleas and wouldn't listen and drank his cans, Mark ended up throwing his cans and apologised for being weak.

I left it and a day later Paul came up to me, it wasn't to say sorry, I don't think that word was in his vocabulary and his whole attitude was that he wasn't responsible for anything, ever! It was pointless even saying anything half of the time because he'd never admit to any wrong doing.

Paul would talk to me about Cath, Jacob, Paul Junior and even his first Wife Pauline. He told me he still loved Pauline and that she was his first love. To my understanding, he had a lot of respect for Cath and he mentioned his second Wife Wendy quite a bit too.

Paul used to tell me he hated his sister Kay though. He told me it was because when his parents, Walter and Betty, passed away that she got everything and was left everything, he told me she literally had the house stripped and everything sold and he was left with nothing so he said he would never forgive her for that.

When Paul and I came to leave Field Head in June 2001 we exchanged mobile numbers and kept in touch, we weren't in touch a lot not until I bumped into him in town in 2003 and he was homeless by then. So, me being how I am said he could come to live with me. I was married at the time with two kids but I couldn't see him on the street. I've taken in many people who were homeless and at that time I was there for my friend Paul and I tried to give him a break. I've always felt compassion for people and I've tried to help any way that I can, I don't like to see people hurting or being sad.

Emotionally Paul wasn't in a good place at all in 2003but I'll say one thing for him, as down as he was he never spoke negatively in any way. Paul used to sing the song "Always look on the bright side of life" all day, it was his motto in life, he wouldn't talk down but he used to talk a lot about dying and how he would be remembered.

I don't think Paul was born the way he was I think he was made. He used to tell me how he loved his Mum and Dad dearly but he'd always struggled because he knew how they had brought him up was wrong! He used to say he couldn't admit it to himself because if he did it would be like speaking badly of the parents he loved. Paul used to say his Mum wanted him to be a Doctor but his Dad wanted him to be a Boxer, his Mum wanted him to stitch them up and his Dad wanted him to kill them. Paul said that even at 2, his Dad would call him over and then he'd punch him and Walter would say "That'll make you a man". When you bring a child up like Paul like how he said Walter and Betty had brought him up there was bound to be something amiss with him wasn't there?

I think Paul had a broken heart and that he was lost soul. His heart broke for the way he was and the life he'd had and yet he spoke a lot of the love he had for his parents, he said he respected them both even though by then they'd both gone.

When I brought Paul home to live with me that first time in 2003 he was very agitated, I'm not sure if it was the drink or the lack of it that day. He wasn't very mobile by then either so he couldn't climb my stairs to go to bed and he didn't really want to get bathed. I showed him around the house and we had another room downstairs and I put a bed in there for him and he slept in there. He was so agitated that first night though that I gave him some Amitriptyline because I was on tablets then and the next day he said to me that he'd had the best night's sleep he'd ever had.

The first night that Paul stayed at my house he was as quiet as a mouse and within the first week Paul and I talked a lot, Paul talked and talked and talked some more, I thought I talked a lot but he was on another level. He told me he just wanted me to listen to him. I could just feel his pain and I could see he was hurting and he needed to get it off his chest. He did have so much agony inside of him.

Paul was writing a sequel to Sweet Agony and he started to write that while he was staying with me at my house. He was quite determined he wanted it finished before he died. I think he knew he wasn't going to be much longer on this earth by the way he was drinking himself to death.

I wouldn't allow him to drink at my house though so he didn't, he was on the wagon the whole time he stayed. One thing I must tell you about that time was that he was always very polite and respectful always. He used to say to me "Janet I'll never take any liberties while I'm living under your roof", it used to anger him quite a lot if he thought people were taking liberties he would say that often, he just wouldn't stand for it.

Paul told me he had been abused as a child and he was talking about sexual abuse although he wouldn't go into detail about it he said it happened at least twice by two different people. There's no wonder he was a bag of confusion, he was broken, struggling and he was hurting but he had no guidance. The two occasions Paul spoke about the sexual abuse he said it was definitely two separate incidents and thinking back to what he told me he said it was in his early teens, between the ages of 11 – 14 at a time when he was vulnerable and just discovering his sexuality.

From my personal experiences with Paul I would never had said he was bi-sexual because he was a proper womaniser, but I think a lot of men that are big, in your face type womanisers are harbouring secret revelations about themselves and their homosexual tendencies, their feelings and their thoughts.

Paul used to tell me his Dad used to beat him for any side of him his Dad thought was feminine or any weakness' that Paul showed, he told me he had a lot of anger towards his parents because of some of the things they used to say to him.

Paul felt a lot of jealousy towards his younger Sister Kay. He told me she screwed his Mam and Dad for money, he felt hatred for her because she was left money in their Wills while he had nothing, it hurt him and it tore him up that they did that. He said that when he lost his parents just twelve weeks apart in 1998 that he was in a bad place mentally and drinking extra heavily, if there even was such a thing for Paul Sykes. He said there was a police presence to keep him from going to one of his parent's funerals, I can't remember which one but he did tell me he wasn't allowed to attend so he spent the day drinking. Paul had feelings and emotions and that was towards his Mam and Dad.

I didn't see Paul Sykes like a lot of people did, I saw so much more and that was the thing that made the difference I think. I saw his anger, saw his propensity and if people have said that Paul was a sexual deviant in prison then it doesn't surprise me one iota because of his experiences of sexual abuse, I do think it was a deviancy rather than a bi-sexual tendency if that makes sense, I think it was more about power, control and domination for him.

It's only the Jesus in me that allows me to love Paul and to see him completely differently. He reminded me of my own Father in fact, both had a cruel side to them, extremely malicious and nasty.

One day, Paul Sykes Snr brought Paul Sykes Junior round to my house for his hair cutting and my clippers broke half way through, he had half his hair shaved off and had to go and have it finished off at the Barbers, imagine doing that to one of Paul Sykes' kids I thought. That was not long before Paul Jnr committed the murder and went to prison.

Paul sometimes came back to my house drunk, but he wasn't allowed in if he was in a state, he would sleep in the front garden instead. I came home one day to see him sat in my garden with a heroin addict, I remember thinking please lord don't let him be bringing everyone back here. I lived at St John's in Wakefield which was classed as one of the posher areas of town I suppose. Looking back, I suppose I brought the tone right down around there when Paul was sleeping in my garden, there was many mornings I would wake up and throw open the curtains to see Paul Sykes fast asleep on my grass. He wouldn't even knock on the door if he'd had a drink but like he said to me many times "Jan I'll never take a liberty", I used to then let him in the house in the morning.

Paul used to love cooking, he loved to go food shopping and we'd go to Leeds market together, he would show me where to get the really good meat from. He showed me how to make a roux to make a sauce, mine always went lumpy but he taught me the proper way.

Paul also taught my daughter how to speak properly because she had a dummy he'd say to her "put ya tongue between ya teeth", she still remembers that to this day. Sometimes when he'd had a drink, he wouldn't be drunk but he used to ask to take my little lass to the shops with him. I was wise though, I never let him. Not that I thought he would do her any harm but she was only about 3 and you can never be too careful with kids, she could have ended up anywhere.

When all the young lads used to bully Paul and pick on him in town they were no better than he was, they were just following the same path, yet foolishly they thought they were better because they thought they were getting one over on Paul Sykes. A good few times he would come back to my house with cuts and bruises from the hidings he'd had from them. He'd come to mine all blistered from where he'd been set on fire, they broke his arm and they'd often take his money off him. It was so unkind, it was wrong no matter who you are, I don't care about Paul's background he was a person and I'll know they'll be those that say that Paul Sykes hurt people also but there's no excuse for that kind of behaviour from anyone. Are any of us perfect?

I know Paul Sykes was a good person, he was broken, abused and lived his life in a world of pain himself.

Paul spoke to me about the fight he had with the American Dave Wilson in which Paul nearly killed him, he spoke to me at length about that. He said it screwed him up for a long time after emotionally and mentally, he just couldn't come to terms with what had happened and it was that fight that finished his boxing career he told me that. It tormented him to the end of his days and he often wondered how he was and if he was still about, other than that Paul didn't really like talking about his boxing career, he wasn't proud of it at all.

In many ways, Paul was like a lost little boy just wanting someone to look after him and for that part my mothering instinct wanted to look after him, sometimes I just wanted to fold Paul up in my arms and be able to take all his pain away.

My relationship with Paul broke down in 2006, a year before he died. I'll tell you the reason why, Paul had been paid a fair bit of money and he wanted to treat me and my Husband to some meat from Leeds Market because we'd been feeding him and he was insistent that he wanted to treat us to this dinner. So, Paul took me to Leeds market again and he loved it, he was saying "Hiya" to all these people he knew that were coming up to speak to him. When we got back to the house Paul said he wanted to go out for a drink, just a couple before dinner but this same evening I was going to the theatre to watch The Rocky Horror Picture Show and before I went I had asked Paul to watch the Rocky Horror DVD with me at home. Paul had this thing about gay people, bi-sexuals and transsexuals, it used to infuriate him he used to get really angry about them. I kept saying to Paul that It was just a laugh and a joke and that we should watch it together but he lasted about half an hour effing and blinding throughout and then he wouldn't watch anymore of it and he went out on the booze instead. As I was going to the theatre to watch Rocky Horror I had got dressed up in a Basque, suspenders and a feather boa, people often dress up to go and watch it. As I was waiting for my friends to come and pick me up Paul came back to the house off his head wanting to be let in, well firstly, I wasn't going to let him in because he was drunk, he knew I was very strict about that and secondly my friends would be there any minute and I would have to open the door and I didn't particularly want Paul to see me dressed up like I was. So, I told Paul to go away and he said to me "Aye I'll go away but give me my meat then, it's mine" we argued for what seemed like an age then suddenly with no warning he put a pole through my front door, that was the only time Paul had shown any violent side to him whilst he had been at mine.

I did eventually get to go to see The Rocky Horror Picture Show, after Paul left with his meat in a plastic bag and I'd cleaned up all the glass. A couple of days later Paul came back to our house and apologised to my husband, not me though and I was the one he'd done that to. I was the one there when he smashed through the door not my husband, he wasn't there yet. Paul was showing him respect and a total lack of it for me but then for some strange reason he didn't have respect for women. That was one of the things I saw in Paul towards the end, he was very derogatory about Women in general. In Paul's eyes, I didn't deserve an apology yet my husband did!

The next time I saw Paul it was when he came with Paul Sykes Junior to pick some of his belongings up and then off he went and I never saw him for a good while after that.

Paul often spoke about dying, we used to have a lot of serious heartfelt conversations about it, he would often ask if I thought a lot of people would go to his funeral. I used to tell him I didn't know but that I'd be there and you know what, I actually wasn't! I didn't have any knowledge that he had died until weeks after he'd been buried. In all honesty after the day that Paul smashed my front door in our relationship was never the same, we were all right with each other but it wasn't the same.

Paul once bought me a present, or so I thought, and when I look at it even to this day it makes me laugh. When Paul was stopping at my house he walked in one day and pulled this ornament from his coat pocket, he knew I liked figurines as I used to collect them, he'd brought me a tall wooden figurine of a man and a woman embracing and it was beautiful. He said, "I've bought this for you Jan and wherever I am, whatever happens to me I want you to look at this and smile, it's for you to remember me by!". I still have it do this day and it does still make me smile when I look at it. I believe that Paul was saying to me "When I die I want this to remind you of me". He didn't want to die but he knew he was dying and it would only be a matter of time. I loved the ornament it would have been something I would have bought myself. I told Paul he was stupid spending his money on me but he didn't realise he had left the price label on it which said £54.99, well I knew that Paul didn't have that kind of money and as it transpired he had been walking around The Pine Shop in Wakefield near Kirkgate Station. Paul had seen it and thought I'd like it so had put it in his jacket and walked out without paying for it the flipping rascal ha ha. It was touching though even though he stole it, I do believe in my heart that if he'd have had the money he would have bought it for me, he knew it would be special to me, he didn't just nick anything, not that I'm trying to justify it because it was wrong to steal it.

Paul used to suffer badly with arthritis and he was in a lot of pain some days, particularly in his hands. He'd play on this with me and he tried to manipulate me to give him Amitriptyline all the time, he was a devil like that, but I got wise to him in the end and would give him placebo's and he wouldn't be any the wiser, it was better than antagonising him and saying no.

It's very true that Paul turned to Jesus towards the end of his life in fact Paul used to carry a bible in his pocket. He studied the bible while he was at my house and we used to go to the Baptist church together sometimes. He would heckle in church sometimes if he'd had a drink but that church loved him unconditionally and they treat him well and I think it was that unconditional love that kept him going back. He came with me to the church I used to go to sometimes called New Horizons in Dewsbury. I was a bit cautious taking him because I was worried that if he started they wouldn't know how to handle him or what to do with him.

He would often talk to me about God in conversations we had and he asked God into his life but he didn't know how to walk with him because he was just too damaged, he was completely broken.

If he had lived long enough I think he might have managed to clean up his act, I know the power of Jesus, Jesus can do anything but it takes our will, only we can choose. I believe God didn't want to see Paul suffering anymore and called him home at the age of 60.

In my opinion Paul Sykes' life was destroyed before it really even began as a child. It was as if he was created, he was made, God didn't create him to have the childhood that he did have, the devil stole him. Paul was always that tormented in his own mind and in my opinion from what Paul told me it was down to his parents. Paul told me his Dad was ridiculously abusive and his Mother was emotionally detached.

I would sum Paul Sykes up with the words lost, broken, desperate, hurting and crying out to be accepted for who he was not what he was made out to be by the people of Wakefield. As long as his reputation was building he felt he had to keep living up to it, even when he didn't feel like he wanted to it was almost as if he was obliged to.

Paul had a good heart I saw it many times, the things he told me about how he felt, I saw him cry many many times at and they were always real tears. I loved Paul, absolutely loved him as a close friend. I was never attracted to him but I could see how women were in his heyday. He had a cocky arrogance about him that he thought he could have had any girl that he wanted.

Paul told me a lot of stories from the years gone by but in the time when I knew him from 2001 to 2006 he never had any girlfriends and I don't think he was interested in those five years.

Paul said to me that even as a child he lived on red alert and that was because of his Father, Paul always had to be ready to defend himself, he could never fully relax and just be a child. He was on guard about his Father and then on guard with the rest of the world. Those that hated him created a monster.

The way he was treat by some people in Wakefield wasn't good so he was more a less saying that if they treat him as a monster then that is what they were going to get, he lived up to the reputation that they were giving him and that wasn't the real Paul Sykes that I knew, he was a sensitive bloke living in a world of hurt.

In all the years that I knew Paul I had never known him to tell lies, all those tales about him swimming across the straits of Johor, he really did that!

Paul had a very sadistic side to him and a very big ego. I believe Paul was narcissistic and certainly had a personality disorder; it was like he had a split personality.

Paul lived the life he did because he didn't know how to get out of it, he'd have never moved away from Wakefield though it was his home and he loved the place.

Paul Sykes' name will always be around in Wakefield folklore forever more, he's infamous and notorious, love him or hate him you'll always remember the name of the marmite character.

One day, my husband and I had a furious argument and I was really upset, I'd been praying and I heard the front door, it was Paul, he was tipsy but not off his head drunk. Anyway, I told him I was so glad to see him, I put my arms around him and hugged him and he just seemed to freeze, he gently pushed me away picked me up at arm's length and placed me back down away from him. I don't think he was used to people being tactile with him and it made him feel a little uneasy and he seemed scared of emotion. I had always been the strong one throughout our friendship, I was always there for Paul and the fact that that day I was vulnerable and needed him for a shoulder to cry on, he just couldn't cope with it emotionally; it was all too much for him.

I don't want to big Paul Sykes up because he did some bad things and he himself knew deep down that he was a wrong un and he didn't like that side of himself, then there was part of him that did, he liked the power he had of scaring people just by giving them a look. If you acted scared of him he'd exploit that but if you stood up to him he respected that. If you were real with him he would be real with you.

I've always said it would have been better if he'd stayed in prison, it kept him off drink and away from bad habits, it was prison life that helped him keep that balance if you like, he was very much institutionalised.

Whilst Paul stayed with me he enjoyed the fact that is was peaceful and calm and he wanted to write the sequel to Sweet Agony, he wanted it finished but he could never stay off the drink long enough to get it done, it was that and the fact that he was in pain quite a bit with his hands. He would always say to me "Always in pencil Jan" he always wrote with a pencil.

As bad as Paul's life was towards the end he still never complained, he used to say that was his lot and to always look on the bright side of life.

To have regrets you've got to know responsibility and accountability, haven't you? Well I do think that's why he drank like he did. In the early days, Paul drank because it's the thing you do as a young guy but at the backend of his life he did it to block the pain out of his childhood, I know the pain he spoke to me about and I know it was to cover the pain in his heart. He wouldn't let Jesus find him. We as people must give Jesus our freewill but Paul wouldn't face up to his past and he chose to drink to numb the pain.

Paul would tell me that he would come into a lot of money now and again but he would squander it all, he said he'd lived the high life, he'd had everything and he'd had nothing, money didn't mean anything to him.

When I think of Paul he makes me smile, when I look at pictures of him I see that sadness at it makes me sad, I can't help feeling a love towards him and a compassionate love for him, a bit of empathy and I think Paul would be so made up that someone is writing books about him now that he's gone.

# JULIE ALLOTT

Julie Allott is local to Wakefield and grew up in the Wakefield area.

Julie went to Newcastle University in 1984 when she was 18 to gain her first degree in Social Studies which took her three years. After gaining that degree Julie decided to train as a Solicitor and attended Leeds Polytechnic she began her career in Law as a trainee solicitor in 1991.

Julie said she really didn't have any intentions to stay local once she had finished her studies and had thought about perhaps moving further South but she applied for a position as a trainee solicitor at a Wakefield firm of Solicitors and 26 years later Julie is still practicing as a Solicitor in Wakefield.

Julie was aware of me as she'd read Unfinished Agony, which I'm pleased to say she thought was excellent! I sat and listened to Julie as she told me what she knew of Paul Sykes.

\*       \*       \*       \*

I used to hear the name Paul Sykes when I started to venture into Wakefield's city centre pubs as a teenager, this will have been around 1982. Growing up in Wakefield I can't really remember a time when I hadn't heard of Paul he was one of those characters that you'd overhear people talking about, he had a reputation and what you heard would give you an idea of what he was about.

When Paul walked in to a pub you would see people leave or pretend that they hadn't seen him, people definitely did not want to make eye contact with him for fear of his reaction, although you were certainly a lot safer being around Paul if you were female!

Paul Sykes' Father Walter sold handkerchiefs and towels door to door for a time. Old Walter used to come around with a suitcase and I remember my Grandmother buying various items from him over the years. My Grandmother told me that she remembers talking to Walter and him saying that he wouldn't be coming around anymore as he'd been having trouble with his Son and he was due out of Prison.

The first time I ever encountered Paul myself was around 1992 and it was because he was the subject of an injunction order. Paul had already breached the court order, though in those days it wasn't a criminal offence to breach a County Court Injunction Order but if you did the court had the power to commit to Prison so you'd have to go along to the court to apply for a committal. The Solicitor I was working with at the time, who is now retired, was well known for being a very feisty woman who dealt with Divorces and Injunctions so it was up to her to go to the court and apply for him to be committed to prison. I went along with her as part of my training just to observe how it was dealt with. On that occasion, I remember Paul was very philosophical about it, he wasn't kicking or screaming and making a big deal of it, from my recollection he took it in his stride and was let off with a warning so he didn't go to prison for it that time.

Over the years I met him an awful lot of times as I worked in the Magistrates Court in Wakefield.

I qualified as a Solicitor in 1993 but I was never to represent Paul Sykes himself although I did go on to act for several people known to Paul. A gentleman called John Batty represented Paul. John Batty was old school and knew Paul well from when he was the man about town right through to his awful decline into less fortunate days.

Paul did have a real go at me one day, he really went for me, I can't remember the exact year but I was representing someone and during the course of the proceedings the court refused bail despite my best efforts and remanded the defendant in to the custody of the court. Paul saw this as my fault and wasn't happy with me at all. The second he laid eyes on me after the hearing he was horrible to me and I mean really horrible, he was really abusive saying that it was all my fault and that I hadn't done my job properly.

Bizarrely, many years later at a point in his life when he was really down on his luck, he was receiving ASBO on top of ASBO and breaching them regularly and he was getting abused and taken advantage of by youngsters, I saw Paul and I remember this encounter vividly as he said to me "Oi I owe you an apology", I was completely taken aback, flabbergasted in fact but I asked him what for and he told me "Because I had a right go at you over one of my lads years ago and it wasn't your fault Julie". He'd remembered the incident very clearly and he went on to say that he knew how I had tried my best for the kids on the estates and that they loved me for what I had done for them. I suppose looking back that that was quite something, to get an apology from Paul Sykes, especially being a woman, well it was almost unheard of!

What I will say about Paul Sykes is this, when Paul was sat in the court corridors he was a constant source of entertainment, he could often be heard singing 'Always look on the bright side of life' and when he was on form he was the wittiest most amusing man you'd ever wish to meet. He was very funny and extremely well read, he'd often talk about literature with me and also Bible quotes that he had memorised, there won't be many that know this but Paul knew the Bible very well.

Paul would love to speak about Charles Dickens he would mention other great writers but he would tell me Charles Dickens was his favourite.

Paul had a tremendous sense of pride in writing Sweet Agony, it brought him a great sense of accomplishment I could tell that, I had read it and had asked him to sign my copy of it one day I regret that I never got this done.

After Paul Junior had been remanded and charged with the murder of Michael Gallagher in 2004 Paul Sykes Jnr was asking to see Paul Snr outside the magistrates. I recall speaking to Paul Snr that day with words to the effect of that his Son needed him right then and that if he couldn't visit then to remember to write to him and support him. Paul turned to me and said, "That boys nothing to me now he's taken a life" I remember being really shocked by his words that day.

Paul Sykes used to always joke to me that I must have made a pact with the devil, this was because every time he saw me I never looked any older he said, he knew how to flatter you when he wanted something.

Towards the end of Paul's life, it was extremely sad to see someone look as broken as he looked. Whatever he did or however he treated people (I've heard the stories) the state that he ended up in towards the end of his life was just tragic. At a time in his life when many are looking forward to how their lives have slowed down and some even looking forward to retirement, Paul had become a tramp! He was homeless, he was unkempt and people would take advantage of him daily.

Paul would often ask me for money when I saw him at Court and I would tell him that I would never give him money but that I'd buy him a warm drink and something to eat. He was always grateful and I enjoyed listening to him. He used to tell me all kinds of stories and sometimes he used to rabbit on a bit, he would often lose the thread of what he was talking about in the first place and he would also come out with his mind-blowing philosophies.

I used to say to Paul that he needed to get all these things down in another book and he'd tell me it was in hand but realistically he was never going to get one done.

I heard that Paul had written another book called 'The Leopards of Maplethorpe' I've been told that Paul's third Wife Cath has it but then I've also been told that it doesn't exist so who knows!

When I think back to the Paul Sykes of 1982/83 he was always smartly dressed and very imposing, his reputation went before him and that had nothing to do with his boxing.

I knew a lot of Police Officers that would talk about Paul. Quite a lot of ex Police Officers ended up working in the Magistrates when they'd retired. Colin Thistlewood an ex Officer used to tell all kinds of stories of Paul and his best friend Burkey.

If you were to look at Paul's criminal record in the early days you would see that most of it was for serious violence whereas towards the end it was all petty offending really, things like Drunk and Disorderly or breaching his ASBO's. Even people with the hardest of hearts would feel quite sorry for him because they had witnessed just how far he had fallen.

Paul Sykes was a highly intelligent and an extremely charismatic man but I will openly admit that I felt intimidated in his company because it was clear for anyone to see that he had an aura of menace coming from him in abundance. Toward the end though it was never like that and I'd like to think that later in his life he had some respect for me and he was always pleasant to me, except for that one time that I have mentioned earlier.

Paul Sykes is, in my opinion, the most notorious character to come from Wakefield, certainly in the last 50 years. I wouldn't put the blame for Paul's behaviour on his father's shoulders, Walter was very much a product of his time from what I've heard.

When Paul passed away my overwhelming thoughts of him was what a waste, what a waste of the potential that he had both in boxing and as an author. It was big news in Wakefield but it came as a surprise to no one I'm afraid to say.

I had never seen him be physically violent with my own eyes but I did see him being nasty to people, getting aggressive and pointing in their faces, that same man I'd seen sleeping in shop doorways and wandering the town looking like an utterly broken man.

# GARY MILLS

Gary Mills is 53, from Lupset, Wakefield and works within the British Prison system. It was Kenny Williams who suggested that I speak to his friend Gary Mills as in his words "Poor Gaz used to come home with lumps and bruises most nights because he was Paul's carer". I imagine that was one hell of a job so I rang Gary and he had a chat with me about his old 'sparring partner' Sykesy.

*     *     *     *

I used to hear the name Paul Sykes when I was very young, I was maybe about 12 years old the first time that I can remember hearing about him. Paul Sykes was notorious in Wakefield when I was growing up. The stories I would hear about him were always bad ones, everything was bad about Paul, no one ever had anything good to say about him and probably rightly so at that time as he was in his prime.

When he was on the out he was usually spending his time carrying out acts of violence and this would be on a daily basis. That's the sort of thing I would hear as a young lad anyway.

The first time I met Paul I'd have been maybe 14/15 years old. I used to knock about with a lad called Stuart Sellers and his Dad used to be Paul's best friend. Stuart's Dad was called Mick Sellers and he was a Wrestler. So, on this particular day when I met Paul I was playing in Stuarts back garden and Stuart and Mick were trying to fix a lawn mower. They were always messing about with cars and car engines normally. Paul Sykes turned up and was asking Mick what was up with the lawn mower so Mick replied, "the piston has gone on it Paul", Paul looked up at me and said "Ooohh if I caught you in the bushes your piston would be knackered". Like I said earlier I was only in my early teens and it shocked the hell out of me, looking back it's quite scary as it was well known that Paul was "The other way" in Wakefield, particularly when he was in Prison. I've heard many stories on Paul Sykes and he would come out with things like that to lads quite often, so that was my first experience of meeting him.

Over the years I saw Paul walking in pubs and he would empty the place within minutes of getting in there. He'd often just pick up some random persons pint and start drinking it and if they dared to say anything about it then they got a clout for their trouble.

I have a couple of brothers who are police officers and they were very familiar with Paul Sykes. One of them was a policeman in Wakefield and had a nasty confrontation with Paul. Paul had carried out a robbery on Ledger Lane Post Office in Outwood, Wakefield. Paul was still in there with an accomplice when my brother was called to the scene to catch the thieves in action. My brother went around the back of the Post Office but it was really dark and he couldn't see a thing. My brother was looking about trying to accustom his eyes to the dark and to get his bearings when 'BANG' the back door flew open and he saw these two blokes running out. My brother instinctively went into police mode and rugby tackled the biggest one which happened to be Paul Sykes. Unfortunately, this was at a time when Paul was in peak physical condition and Paul got straight up and with one punch broke both my brother's cheek bones, nose, jaw and put his teeth through his bottom lip as well as losing some teeth, he also damaged his eye socket and all those injuries came from just one punch. Rather foolishly my brother got up and rugby tackled Paul again this time managing to put him in cuffs and arrest him, his mate got away though. He gave my brother all this trouble and my brother wasn't small standing at 6ft 6'.

The write up in the paper said Paul Sykes had said in court "I got caught but I must commend the police officer because I didn't think he was gonna get up from that punch so fair play to him"!

Many years later I used to work at a place in Wakefield with high priority offenders. Many were murderers and sex offenders but Paul Sykes was brought to our attention purely because he was such a prolific offender. At this time, it was 2004/05 and Paul had definitely seen better days, he was living his life mostly on his back due to the drink and he was in the papers on a weekly basis for one offence or another, usually getting an ASBO or because some kids had set fire to him whilst he slept.

Paul didn't live in the place that I worked but it was mentioned from higher up the chain that it was about time that something was done and that we should take up the challenge of finally helping to sort Paul Sykes out. So, my manager came to see me and my colleagues and said that we were thinking of a project to somehow help Paul once and for all. My boss asked us all personally if we thought we could help him. The rest of my team shied away from the idea but I put myself forward and as I'd known of Paul for many years and told them that I would do it. At the time Paul was in Armley prison in Leeds but he was due to be released, thinking back it could quite possibly have been the last time he spent in custody.

So, it was all sorted, myself and a probation officer called Dan Munroe went to pick Paul up at the prison gates on the morning of his release. Dan was from Lawfield Lane Probation Office and he'd known of Paul for years. Dan actually offered to help Paul for nothing, he wasn't doing it as part of his job he just wanted to finally see Paul get sorted.

At this point in his life, the Paul of old had long gone and he wasn't really capable of beating people up like he had once done as he was always drunk and wasn't by any means in the best of health but I dare say even then if he'd have got hold of you you'd have still had a bit of trouble on your hands.

So, me and Dan were given the job of supporting Paul. Because of the position he'd got his life in to Paul was then more of a public nuisance and his biggest crimes at that time were shouting at passers-by or getting ridiculously drunk and wandering into zones of the city that he had been barred from by the Courts. The Courts had just got sick of seeing him so I think that was another reason that this project had been put into place. There was that and the fact that people had started to take advantage of him, like I said, he was set fire to and beaten up and kicked on a regular basis so he desperately needed this project and sooner rather than later. Obviously, he also needed help with his alcohol abuse, we'd been trained to help people with this problem and we knew that it would greatly benefit Paul otherwise we would have been wasting our time.

After some time of Dan and I looking after Paul a gentleman called Ernest Hibbert from CAP (Community Awareness Programme) came on board to help Paul too. It turned out that Ernest used to go to Snapethorpe School with Paul and knew him right well so us three got together and we built a team around Paul. We had someone from housing who got him a flat on the new Scarborough Estate near Peacock, we got him a G.P. because no other GP's would touch him because he had caused so much chaos in practices over the years with his bad behaviour. We made a big effort to get his quickly declining health sorted out but we also watched his alcohol intake. Paul would drink as much as he could get his hands on in any one day so we had money to get Paul some drink, as it would have been dangerous for him to just halt it completely all at once. We would buy a crate of twenty-four then we would give Paul eight cans a day. We bought him his favourite Calsberg Special Brew of course.

When we first put all this into place for Paul he was drinking fifteen to twenty cans of nine percent Special Brew a day. I never remember ever seeing him drinking water. The only thing he used water for was to bath in and he didn't do that very often. Gradually we got his alcohol intake down to five cans of Kestrel a day but I knew Paul was still going out scrounging money to buy extra drink too.

We came across a guy called Stephen Whitely, Steve still walks around Wakefield town and is still sleeping rough to this day. Steve had known Paul for years and the team and I came across him at Paul's. Paul must have met him in town and brought him back to his for a good drink. Well it turned out this Steve was looking for somewhere to live, so we set up for Steve to move in with Paul to keep an eye on him when we weren't there. It was a handy arrangement for all concerned. Steve used to sleep on the sofa and it did last for quite a while, that was until

Paul stabbed Steve in the arse with a pair of scissors!!

Steve used to cook for Paul and he stayed living with him for well over a year. Steve was really patient with Paul and put up with him when most other people would have thrown in the towel. Paul didn't realise that Steve living there was a godsend for him because if it hadn't been for Steve cooking for him he would have barely eaten anything at all. He did a good job of looking after Paul and made sure that Paul remembered to at least wash.

The day I dreaded finally happened though. Ernest and I went around to Paul's flat to be told by a neighbour that something had happened in the house. To cut a long story short, an argument had developed between Paul and Steve and Paul picked up a pair of scissors and stabbed poor Steve in the arse. Paul was arrested for that and charged but Steve dropped the charges.

This is what was reported on 28th of April 2006 in the Wakefield Express. The headline was 'Ex-boxer on stab charge': -

"Former Heavyweight boxer Paul Sykes appeared in court on Tuesday to face a charge of Wounding with Intent. Sykes, 59, of Alverthorpe Road spoke to confirm his name, date of birth and address before the alleged charge of Unlawfully Wounding Stephen Whiteley with intent to do him Grievous Bodily Harm was read out. The offence was said to have taken place on Friday, April 14th. District Judge Jonathan Bennett sent the case to Leeds Crown Court to be heard at a later date and released Sykes on conditional bail. In 1979 Sykes fought John L Gardner for the British and Commonwealth Boxing titles. During his heyday Sykes toured extensively across America with flamboyant U.S. Boxing Promoter Don King."

In all the time we were looking after Paul, that was the only time he'd been in trouble. Paul, at that time, had been so quiet and I know that my brothers on the West Yorkshire Police force wondered where the hell he'd gone as they'd had no trouble from Paul in months

I left the firm whilst Paul was still alive but one of the last things I did for him was tried to re-introduce him to his estranged family. The idea was to organise a meeting with Cath and his kids, it never happened while I was still around him but I heard that it did happen after I'd left. Paul had been estranged from his family for many years. He would often get the idea that he wanted to go and see them but then he'd have a drink and just forget the idea and get drunk. He had real trouble remembering anything because of what he was drinking. He did tell me many times that he wanted to see them though but he also had no wish for them to see him the way he was. Paul knew exactly how far down he'd fallen but he was past caring at that point. I dread to think what Paul would have been like if we hadn't given him the support we did.

I spent hours talking to Paul at times, I'd pass whole days in his flat just making sure he was alright. What I learnt first-hand from spending so much time with him was that he wasn't the thick thug that people portrayed him to be. He was a fantastically intelligent person who could talk about any subject in the world that you cared to bring up. He would say that people always talked about doing things or going places. Well, one of Paul's favourite sayings was "I wouldn't talk about it I'd have just got off me backside and went".

He used to tell me how he'd seen the mountains of Russia. Paul used to tell me a story many times about how he once went to a party in Singapore that was being held in a big hotel. Paul went thinking it was all paid for and it was all free for him but it turned out that it wasn't and the people there were chasing Paul for a hell of a lot of money because of the bill he had racked up whilst partying in there. So, Paul was getting chased by the Singapore Police and he dived in the river to escape and started to swim, after a short while of him swimming he noticed what he thought were bullets hitting the water round about him. He said it felt like he was getting pelted on both sides. It turned out that it was bloody fish trying to bite him. He said when he thought he was getting shot at it was actually these small sharks snapping at him. It's funny because people laughed at him on the TV documentary saying that he had swum with sharks across the Straits of Johor but he really did. He even told me tales of when he went to China.

Paul used to talk about the American Dave Wilson whose career he ended. That always played on Paul's mind I think. He told me he was remorseful for the poor fella and that he wished he'd have been allowed to box sooner as a pro. He just told me that he couldn't help doing the things on the side that would get him into trouble. He had massive regrets in his life. He would mention John L Gardner quite a lot. Paul's views on that fight were that after three rounds he just lost interest. He told me that John L was hitting him with punches that he'd never been hit with in his entire life. He said Gardner's punches were not that hard but that they were nonstop and coming in from all different angles. He told me that by round three he had just had enough and shamefully he turned his back on him. Paul often told me that he should have beaten Gardner but he never took him seriously enough. He said he drank a lot in the build up to that fight and he thought that because he had a good thump on him that Gardner wouldn't get past three rounds and he'd go down. When really John L Gardner was the first proper boxer that could take Paul's power. He knew his game was rumbled in the fourth round when Gardner was still in front of him. That was when he realised that he'd well and truly underprepared, those were his words to me.

I must say that I often left Paul's flat with many a lump and bump as when Paul spoke of old stories he would often get quite giddy and carried away and start to carry out the actions of the stories he was recounting about him belting someone. I wasn't too pleased about hearing these stories especially when he started shadow boxing in my face. He'd also re-enact his old fights and tell me what he'd do if his opponents came at him from different angles all the while jigging about with his giant fists pushing into my face. I particularly remember a day when he said "Get up Gaz I wanna show ya how it happened" I told him no chance as he was still a big bloke and he told me "Get up now Lupset" (he had nicknamed me Lupset because that is where I was from) so I reluctantly got up, so he's dancing about and he threw a punch which caught me on the top of my head, "Aaaarrgghh" I shouted, he said to me "Ya silly bastard you were supposed to duck" I told him I hadn't expected him to hit me as I thought he was just showing me, he looked at me and said "What's the point in fighting if you're not gonna belt someone?"

These little spars would often happen particularly when he got carried away. He even punched me in the back of the head once when he was in a bad mood. There would be days he'd tell me he wasn't interested in that day and he'd tell me to fuck off out of the door. To be honest there were a few days like that but this particular day I stood up to him, "Shut up Paul I'm not listening to your shit today" I told him "BANG" at the back of my head, I didn't half feel that one. I think I screamed at him then left him to his own devices, it was clear I wasn't going to get anywhere with him after that.

Most of the time though he couldn't get out of the chair. He'd just sit there smoking one cig after the other. His life, at that point in time was cigarettes and alcohol. When I used to walk in with his cans his face would light up. He'd be sat there grinning rubbing his hands together saying, "Oh you're a good lad" and that would be first thing in the morning, probably no later than 8.30am. Quite often he'd have had a couple by then just to start him off.

Paul's hygiene whilst he was living on the streets had been really bad but when he was in that flat we got him and Steve lived there we really cleaned him up. If Paul was in a light-hearted mood then that day spent with Paul would be a funny one, he had a great sense of humour and on those days, he was great company.

I remember saying to Paul "Do you remember when you did that Post Office on Ledger Lane" he said to me "Yeah I do" I said to him "Do you remember that bobby you thumped?" and with that his eyes lit up, "Ooh aye I copped him with a fucking beauty like, right on the button" I said "That bobby was my brother Paul" he paused for a moment then said "Get out of it, I never thought he was ever gonna get up, I didn't half crack him" Paul was laughing his head off. I told him "It's not funny Paul our kid was out of work for months after that on the sick" but Paul thought it was hilarious. He asked me if my brother was from Lupset and I told him yes, we all were. Paul then said, "You can always tell a lad from Lupset because he can take a punch". Paul told me he had to admire my brother for standing up after that punch.

Paul spoke to me very openly about things and I'll never forget one time when Paul started to tell me how he started writing in Prison. He told me "I've always had a lot to say and I've done a lot but to tell you the truth Gary, that book would never have happened if I'd never fancied the fucking lad who came around and got me in to the education class for it in Durham nick in the 1980's". That's where the idea of writing Sweet Agony had first come from.

Paul liked the younger lads, I should say he never actually told me that himself but I've heard from many sources that had done time with Paul that one of his favourite quotes was "You can have it awake or you can have it asleep". From what Paul did tell me I gathered that it was just something he did whilst he was away in prison. I certainly never heard any stories of Paul up to anything with men when he was out of prison, unless you count that shocking thing he said to me when I was about 14.

In all the time I spent looking after Paul, I don't even think he had any interest in sex. The only thing that seemed to interest him were booze and fags, everything else had left him years ago he would say. He would sit and reminisce about being with Cath and his kids though.

When I was growing up I used to knock about with a lad called John Doggett and his Dad used to work with my Dad. John told me that his sister Wendy had started seeing Paul Sykes. John told me that Paul was a right nasty bastard towards his family and Wendy couldn't cope being with him anymore so she buggered off somewhere when he was in prison so that he couldn't find her. John told me Paul would go to the family home on Oswald Terrace in Lupset with a petrol can demanding to be told where she was or he'd burn the family house down. Wendy's Dad always stood up to Paul and never told him anything but Paul Sykes used to put the Doggett family through hell.

Paul Sykes was bad, mad, articulate and intelligent. That's how I would sum up Paul in my years of knowing him well. Paul was naturally intelligent even at school but he just chose to thump people even as a kid. Then when he got older he liked thumping bouncers who got lippy with him. Paul knew from an early age that he was good at violence and this was the tool he would use the most in his life, his fists rather than his brain.

In the same year that he said that to me about the bushes, well it wasn't long after that that I was round at my mate Stuart Sellers again one night and Paul had come around. He was drunk when he got there and he started arguing with his friends Mick and Janet Sellers. It had started over Paul's boxing trainer at the time because Mick was calling him a useless bastard and Paul wasn't best pleased about it so he went for Mick. Mick being a wrestler he got Paul in a bear hug and with him being ridiculously strong there was no way Paul was getting out of that so he did the only thing that he thought he could do and that was to bite part of Mick Sellers ear off! After that Janet, Micks wife, got a loaded crossbow and fired it at Paul but it missed and hit their big grey truck in the garden. Paul got away unharmed but after that, but for about three weeks, there was a heavy police presence in Lupset. The rumour mill had gone into overdrive and the word was that Paul was going to have Mick killed but nothing happened and it died down.

Paul Often spoke of his son's Paul Junior, who he had with his first wife Pauline and Michael who he had with his second wife Wendy. Paul used to say he couldn't understand how their Michael had turned out the way he had as he had never been allowed to be part of his life from day one. Paul never had any dealing with his son Paul Jnr after he committed the murder of Michael Gallagher in 2004. When Paul Senior would hear anything of Paul Junior he would just shake his head and call him "A useless bastard". The love he had for his son Paul Jnr had all gone after that he would say. Paul said that Paul Jnr was trying too hard to be like him because they had the same name but that that had only got him into trouble. I can fully understand Paul Seniors views on this as I know myself that Paul Junior would often try to tax drug dealers but he would often become unstuck in doing so. He couldn't go the full yard and he would often get himself a good hiding for his trouble, something that didn't happen to Paul Snr as he was obviously a one off.

Very few people were bothered about young Paul he didn't have the same reputation as his father so often didn't get away with behaving the way he did.

Paul often spoke about his other son Jacob, he has Down Syndrome and Paul used to get quite emotional whenever he was speaking about him. He would always tell me how he loved that little boy to bits. He would drink to numb the pain of his separation from them.

One of the things Paul would say quite often to me was "Good or bad they'll never forget the name Paul Sykes". He was right, folk won't forget him even if they despised him.

Paul Sykes stands alone and is unquestionably one of the more famous people from Wakefield along with Jane McDonald.

*"Every argument is going to end in a fight so you may as well fight first"*

**-P Sykes**

# IMRAN HUSSAIN

Imran Hussain is 32 and is from Lupset in Wakefield. Imran now lives in Dewsbury and he contacted me via the Paul Sykes Facebook page to tell me about the many times he and his friends used to go around to Paul's flat on a Friday and Saturday night to drink with the 'Wakey Legend'.

\*     \*     \*     \*

I first heard about Paul Sykes when I was as young as 7 years old. My Auntie and Uncle used to live across the road on Gissing Road in Lupset. I spent many nights at my Auntie and Uncles in around 1993 and my Uncle, who was a big guy himself, used to tell me to avoid playing anywhere near Paul Sykes' house with balls or anything that could cause damage in case I smashed a window of his or something. My Uncle would always seem pretty wary of this man who lived over the road from him. My Uncle had never had any run ins with Paul and Paul would even invite my him over for drinks but my Uncle was always apprehensive about accepting his invitation and didn't ever go across and just preferred to keep it at "Hello" and that's it.

The first time I ever saw Paul wasn't until about 1994. Like I said I'd always been warned to keep my distance from Paul's home and I always did but the first time I saw him wasn't in the street it was when I was in Waterton School's playground and Paul was in someone's back garden which overlooked the school. I became aware that everyone in the playground was drawn towards Paul, everyone seemed to know him and it was like seeing fans flock towards a celebrity. I followed everyone over despite being told to keep away from him and being told he was a dangerous man, I naturally wanted to see what the fuss was about. As I made my way over it was as if Paul was intentionally putting on a show for all of us kids, he was telling jokes and showing off his muscles. It was like he was the local hero.

As soon as one of the teachers noticed what was going on though they were straight over to us and with worried looks were telling us to keep away from Paul. From that day onwards, every time I saw him he would be a little more drunk and unkempt then from the time before.

I would really get to know Paul Sykes better in 2004/05 when I started to drink myself with my friends as lads do. Paul, by that time was renting a house in Alverthorpe from a friend of mine. Me and the lads I used to hang around with needed somewhere we could go to drink so it was handy that Paul used to invite us around to drink with him most weekends.

Even though we all knew who Paul was and we were aware of his bad reputation he didn't seem like a bad person, a bit of an oddball rogue perhaps but he was good fun to be around, I must have drunk with him on at least thirty different occasions.

I was only 18/19 at the time and sometimes there would be up to ten other people in his house. We loved to listen to his stories he'd have us all ears on the edge of our seats listening to some of his escapades.

Health wise Paul was fucked, I can't put it any other way, he was really in a bad way and I remember well him telling me that he hadn't eaten for two weeks, he told me all he did was drink and that the beer kept him fed. He had a poor diet of Special Brew and White Lightening along with the fags that he would smoke nonstop.

His flat was an absolute shit tip and the only place decent to sit down was in his front room as everywhere else was a mess with cups and plates that were strewn about unwashed and the place was damp from several leaks his flat had.

I suppose as young lads we couldn't be too picky in our places to drink, it was either in his flat where at least we were mostly dry or the alternative which would have been to hang around the streets or in parks, where inevitably we'd get moved along all the time and besides, the stories Paul would tell us were out of this world and it was worth sitting in the squalid conditions just to be able to listen to him. He often told us about his various times in Prison and how he would handle it. He always said the way to deal with the screws was to let them know that you'd give them a smack, that way they wouldn't give you any attitude. Those were his exact words and he told me that many times. He always made sure the guards knew that he had the ability to give them a fight. Paul told me he would often shadow box in their faces just to give them something to think about if they ever felt like ambushing him.

Paul also told me about how he went to spar George Foreman once. He said he was stood on one side of the ring and Foreman was stood on the other. Paul told us all that he was thinking in his head "I'm gonna fucking bash this black bastard" but in fact George Foreman gave Paul an absolute hiding. Paul said that he could laugh about it now but that he took a right pounding from big George.

One story he told me that made me laugh was the time he said he'd been to a Detroit gym to spar with Leon Spinks, who was in camp getting ready to face Muhammad Ali. Paul said after the gym he was sat on a sofa in there with Leon Spinks, his brother Michael Spinks and Tommy 'The Hitman' Hearns and they all had a spliff together according to Paul, he said you couldn't make it up!

In the time I spent with Paul, he used to speak very openly about his sexuality and his time behind bars. He was very honest about it all and even used to joke about it to all us young lads saying he fancied us all and he was gonna bum us! We knew it was Paul's sense of humour and none of us felt threatened or at risk in his house. There's no doubt in my mind that he indulged in homosexual activity in because he told us all. He said that was back in the day and that the only interest he had now were cigarettes and booze.

Paul did tell me a story of a man from Wakefield (I won't mention his name), Paul said they'd been stories of Paul forcing himself on this guy but that they were untrue and that it had been 100% consensual and as Paul told me this story the very words out of his mouth were "I knew he wanted it so I gave him it".

He would often tell us we were good looking lads and was open about that and not embarrassed of it in the slightest, he told us he used to love the girls also but not now "Drink is my woman now" he would say. At that time, no woman in her right mind would have looked at him he would say.

We were company for Paul and he would tell us just how much he looked forward to the weekends when we'd go around. He said he loved us Muslims because we had always been kind to him and never judged him.

Paul would often get emotional after a drink and be close to tears while shouting "I love you Paki's" then he'd want to cuddle us. He used the term "Paki's" in a loving manner he never meant it in a hostile way and I'd like to make that clear, he never offended any of us.

The documentary channels were his favourite to watch while he was holed up in his flat, he'd watch them all day. He had a particular favourite which was C.I.S which is a crime drama, he wasn't really a music man when I knew him he just used to have the telly on twenty-four hours a day.

Paul was a huge Mike Tyson fan but one-person Paul detested was an old Sportsman called Les D'Arcy. D'Arcy was from Lupset and I don't know why he had such a dislike for him but Paul would often be heard sat in his chair slagging him off.

Paul was an intelligent man who lived a life that really shouldn't have been a life for him. His life towards the end was a very negative life, it should have had more positives but he destroyed himself with alcohol, fags, drugs and prescription drugs too.

Paul Junior used to live off his Dad's name, but he would try and bully people. Paul Jnr tried to intimidate people but if they stood up to him he would back off, he wasn't an authentic tough guy like his father was that's for sure, in my opinion Paul Junior was a thieving bullshitter and being on heroin was his life and his God. When Paul Jnr committed that murder Paul Sykes Snr disowned him. He would often call him a useless bastard and that all his life he had fought with his fists but that Paul Jnr killed that poor man in a coward's way, he had stabbed Michael Gallagher thirty-three times over 50p and I must agree with his Dad about that. That was Paul Jnr all over, he had nothing about him. I don't ever remember him having a job in his life he was just a 10-bob thief and it's no surprise to many people that he is now serving a life sentence over 50p, because that's what he killed that poor guy for, nothing else. What a waste.

Now and again I remember the times I spent with Paul Sykes in his flat and none of us that went around his flat have bad memories of him, we remember how he'd say, "I love you Paki's you're all good kids" and how he'd tell us of how "Abdul Aziz was the first Paki in Wakefield" he was Paul's best friend years before he would say and he used to tell us he was a somebody in Wakefield.

# LEE DANIELS

Lee Daniels is 32 years old and is a builder from Ossett. Although Lee is not from the same generation as Paul Sykes, Lee used to see a hell of a lot of Paul towards the end of his life.

Lee got in touch with me through the Paul Sykes Facebook page and although this won't be a particularly pleasant read, mainly because it's about Paul's decline, I felt it was relevant and I wanted to put across the full picture of Paul from fit boxer through to his shocking ending.

\*        \*        \*        \*

I grew up in Ossett and many of my generation, particularly at school, used to come out with Paul Sykes quotes from the documentary on YouTube.

Paul Sykes' name was incredibly famous in Ossett where I'm from, I've heard so many times that when Paul was in his prime he would go into the pubs in Ossett and the atmosphere would change as his presence would put everyone on edge. I also heard that he'd touch blokes' Wives in front of their faces to get a reaction, I was told it was one of his favourite things to do. There was a story about a couple of brothers from Ossett called Labourn who doubled up on him after he did this and put him in his place, it was widely known that these brothers could have a tear up!

I wasn't to meet Paul personally until 2004 when my mate moved into a bedsit on Alverthorpe Road and it was directly below Paul Sykes' bedsit, it was on the side of Scuffler's Sandwich Shop.

My friend and I were only 17 at the time, we both used to see him in the street looking slightly worn, big beard, basically looking every part of the tramp that he had become, to be perfectly honest with you. He was always nearly gone, you couldn't get much sense out of him. Whenever we did meet face to face it was because he knocked on the door asking to borrow money from my mate. This happened a lot in the year he lived below Paul. It was never big money, mainly always just a few pounds. If my friend had it to spare he would give it to Paul and I even gave him a couple of quid on occasions just because we both felt so sorry for him.

Sometimes we'd be coming up the road and Paul would be sat on the kerb directly outside the bedsits and he would look up and shout, "It's alright lads I've got money today I don't need owt" he'd have an eight pack of Special Brew for company, every time we gave him money it only ever went on drink.

Often Paul was that far gone that he used to piss down the stairs towards the front door, my friend used to have to tell him off for it, never out of nastiness and when he did tell Paul well, Paul would always be very remorseful and extremely apologetic saying that he couldn't remember doing it. Other than him pissing on my mate's doorstep he was never any trouble to us.

Paul was always very respectful towards me and my mate and he was never nasty or violent in any way. We were just two young lads and sometimes we'd have parties at my friend's bedsit and Paul loved to come in and talk to us young lads, you could tell when he started talking that he was a man of the world, of course it was a bonus that there would be free booze and a few of our mates thought it was dead cool that we lived downstairs from this Wakey legend! He loved an audience and he would tell all us impressionable young lads loads of stories from his younger days.

Paul, by this time, was just a shell of the man that we had all grown up hearing so many tales about. His big greying beard was discoloured from all the fags he smoked, he had a constant glaze in his yellowing bloodshot eyes by then, and I think most of what made Paul Paul had already left him, he was mentally shot and all that remained was a frail weak body that was still somehow being driven along by his soul. I find it quite unbelievable that he managed to live another three years in that state, it is a crying shame!

I also often used to see Paul asleep behind Balne Lane Library near Wakefield Prison. It has been knocked down now and they've built housing on it but that's where Paul used to hang out drinking anything he could get his hands on. I couldn't understand why Paul did this as he had his bedsit on Alverthorpe Road. He also had a Social Worker who was a really sound bloke who used to come around daily to look after Paul and tidy his bedsit up. He was really protective of Paul, he was a stocky powerful looking fella who looked like he could handle himself if he needed to. I think this is what Paul needed at times a body guard type of person if you like.

One Friday me and my mate had been drinking and my mate got all his old FHM magazines out and believe it or not we found the one that Paul had featured in. We went and knocked on Paul's door and gave it to him, he was really chuffed. He had been sat on his own drinking and smoking and I think he was glad of the company. He sat telling us stories about his boxing career and it was clear he had not had any company but his own for a long time, he was in his element. He loved seeing his pictures in the magazine that night and to be quite honest he wasn't a threat to anyone in the weakened state that he was in. Two things that stick with me from that night is firstly, when I gave him a cigarette to smoke he smoked the full fag in just two drags, I'm not exaggerating and secondly, the size of his fucking hands, I've never seen hands as big as his!

Over the year that my friend lived in that bedsit I only ever saw Paul getting visited from two people, one being his Social Worker and the other being his son Adam, who I believe was regularly using Heroin at the time.

There were a few incidents whilst Paul lived there, for instance half a dozen young Asian lads about 17 to 19 in age used to turn up braying on Paul's door screaming for him to go outside, shouting that they were going to kill him. I don't know what that was about but Paul was too afraid to come down to the door. Maybe he had upset them during the day when he'd been out, I never did discover what it was all about. Perhaps they were just after the reputation of being able to say that they had beat up Paul Sykes but it happened several times. I remember another Asian guy, about 40, coming around once and he started slapping all these younger lads telling them to leave Paul alone, it can't have been easy for Paul.

Paul was very subdued most of the time and gormless looking, like he was in a zone and in his own little world. When you looked into his eyes there wasn't much there. He'd given up on life, shuffling around with his six coats on and he was very fearful if he ever had to leave his bedsit. As weak as he became though he still had a good handshake. He's still spoken about in Wakefield, even now.

# DEAN ORMSTON

Dean Ormston is 50 years old and is from Batley. Dean runs Wakey Ink Tattoo & Piercing on Kirkgate in Wakefield and has been there since the Millennium.

*     *     *     *

I heard about Paul Sykes years ago when he was a big thing. I was at a mate's house in Birstall, Batley, it will have been about 1990, when Paul turned up to collect some rent from him. Paul knocked on the door and when my mate opened it Paul said to him in a very hushed tone, "You owe some rent money and I'll be back tomorrow to collect it" and then off he went. I asked my mate who it was and he told me it was Paul Sykes, that he was a debt collector and that he'd just got out of prison. Needless to say, my mate got the rent money together and that was the end of it. That was the first time I had seen Paul.

I would go on to see a lot more of Paul Sykes but it would be out of my tattoo parlour window. Paul would often sit outside my shop on a bench nearby and the first time I saw him there he was about as far removed as you could get from the Paul Sykes I'd seen the first time when he had paid my mate a visit for rent money. I would see him sleeping on that bench for many years with his big beard nestling against his big overcoat. When he wasn't sleeping on the bench he was sat on it drinking cans and bottles. If he was asked to move he wouldn't shift as far as he was concerned that was his bench. The people of Wakefield just got used to him being there and they left him alone. One of the main reasons he sat on that bench in particular was that there was an off license next door and he used to go in there often.

Since Paul died it seems to be the place where all the drinkers now sit and booze, as I speak to you now there are people sat there drinking. Paul just set the trend, right outside my business.

I spoke to Paul on the odd occasion. The off license door is next door to me and I saw him there one morning, he was stood swaying and staggering about and looked at me and growled "What you looking at"? I looked at him and said "You, you fucking has-been" and with that he turned to me and said, "Better a has-been than a never been like you" and to be honest that has stuck in my head, he had a point. He may have been staggering about but he was as quick as ever with his witty comeback and that was only the year before he died!

Looking back Paul wasn't someone that I would take any notice of, I'd see him daily and he ended up just being a part of the furniture. If you passed him you'd hear him mumble a lot.

I once saw him asleep outside the Job Centre and young kids were throwing stones at him as he slept.

It's odd to think that that man I didn't think twice about has now had two books written about him, and with a film and a new documentary being made he's going to be a somebody once again. I watched him the other day on YouTube and he predicted electric cars didn't he and he got that right.

It's sad to say but I used to see Paul literally shitting himself, he used to walk about stinking of it and if the coppers had to come and get him for whatever reason I'd often hear one of them say "I'm not putting him in our car" and they'd walk him down the street to Wood Street nick rather than pollute their car.

It's a massive shame that Paul turned himself into the absolute wreck of a man that he became. If Paul Sykes could have seen his future in 1990, somehow could have seen himself as he ended up he'd have laughed and said 'that ain't me'.

Watching Paul Sykes at Large is like watching Rita, Sue & Bob too, you don't forget it and there's so many quotes from it that stick in your mind like, "What's these lights doing on Cath, turn em off and let your eyes adjust and we're reet now".

Paul has become more famous for being infamous shall we say. He lived his life how he wanted to, until life made him live how he had to. He died at 60 years old, that's no age these days.

# A WAKEFIELD POLICE OFFICER

Name withheld by request

The one thing I would have loved to have included in Unfinished Agony would have been a figure of authority, but against all my best efforts it wasn't meant to be. I had, on several occasions contacted the new police station in Normanton but of course I was always told that they couldn't divulge any information about Paul Sykes due to the Data Protection Act. So, as you can imagine I was thrilled when my good friend Simon Ambler called me one morning to say that he was in the company of an ex Lupset bobby who was happy to speak to me but wanted to remain anonymous as he was still a serving Police Officer but in a different area. I, of course, must respect his wishes.

*     *     *     *

I first heard the name Paul Sykes when I went to an incident on the Lupset estate in 1991. It was at Hall Road shops and Paul had been talking to some girls outside the shop and to be honest he was well oiled in drink. An elderly gentleman named Roy Meek had stopped to warn the girls to stay away from Paul Sykes because he was trouble and that they should get as far away as they possibly could from him. Paul had overhead what poor Roy had said and punched him, he made a right mess of poor old Roy Meek. The impact of that punch split poor Roy's face down the middle. My colleague and I turned up at the scene minutes after this had happened, we had to call an ambulance and get Roy to Pinderfields hospital urgently.

After hitting Roy, Paul walked into Robert Ramsden's shop so we had to send out a Police Inspector and a dog handler to try to coax Paul out of the shop. Paul never went anywhere quietly he always fought or played up in some way. That day the main Police Inspector came, talked him out of the shop and into the van. Paul was then taken to the Wood

Street cells. It was when Paul got there that he started to play up, he loved to put on a show whenever he was in our station. His usual game was to fully cooperate then when we would move onto the next stage of the process he'd back track just to be awkward. Paul often tried to intimidate our officers by squaring up to them. Even if you caught Paul Sykes on a good day and he was compliant you'd still need a team of at least three of us as we never wanted it to get to a point where we were fighting with him because that ended up with officers getting injured. Paul more often than not let us know that he was going to do what Paul wanted to do and in his time not ours, we had to play a silly game with him. Paul would often say "I'm not coming" but then at the 11th hour he'd get up, smile and do what you wanted him to do in the first place.

Believe it or not if you were a time served officer he would have some respect for you. He wouldn't speak to police respectfully unless he thought you were an experienced officer. If he knew you or saw some rank on your shoulder then he would show respect and bow his head. In my opinion, this was because he got on with some Prison Officers and that was down to him being institutionalised, if you had to ask Paul anything it was better to ask him in a polite why, he responded better to that.

There's many police officers on the street who can be a bit rude, but when you get to the police managers, they are far more educated and more understanding so you shouldn't have to get the Chief Inspector out for an assault but basically, they did for Paul Sykes to save injuries to any of the team. I dealt with Paul Sykes so many times in Wakefield usually daily.

In 2003/04 Paul got assaulted himself and I was called out to that. This happened at the bottom of Kirkgate near Wilkinson's roundabout. It was around that time Paul had started looking like a tramp. People knew of Paul's reputation so they took full advantage of this. Paul had diabetes badly and he wasn't looking after himself and I would often see him sleeping rough. I would see him show off to his alcoholic friends, I'd hear him bragging that he could drink more than any of them. When I was called out to Paul's assault what had happened was that Paul had been arguing with a lad a lot younger than he was, and this lad had smacked Paul in the face and broken his jaw. A witness had seen everything and phoned an ambulance as well as the Police.

There was an understanding with the ambulance crews that they would never go to Paul without a police presence because of Paul's past behaviour with them. When I got to the scene the ambulance crew were stood off Paul waiting for us to arrive. We got there and managed to speak with Paul and this time he was ok, he could hardly speak though because of his injury so it would have been painful for him to start shouting abuse at us. We got Paul into the back of the ambulance and I had to stay with him because the ambulance crew refused to take him to Pinderfields without my presence. So, I started talking to Paul and he wanted to know a little bit about me. I told him I had been a life guard in the past and then Paul started to open up to me telling me that he had also been a life guard at one time in Blackpool and that he had once saved someone's life on the beach and that it had been in the papers. He told me he'd got the Silver Cross with distinction because he'd done the highest level you could get whilst being a lifeguard. That just showed Paul could have achieved things when he wanted to. He also knew so much about human anatomy because when I asked him how he knew he'd broken his jaw he said that he had studied it in prison and that he had researched physiology and that he knew he'd broken his mandible bone and he showed me where on his face it was. He told me he knew a thing or two about broken jaws and smiled as much as he could smile.

When Paul was sober he was extremely articulate and intellectual. A good few times I'd watched him in the dock at court talking to the magistrates and he'd be arguing the points of law and quite often Paul would be in the right. The thing with Paul Sykes was that he'd been through the system that many times he was your nightmare defendant really. Paul would often defend himself on occasions and if he wasn't defending himself his lawyer of choice was John Batty of Wakefield. As long as you remembered to let Paul have his say he would be reasonable with people.

It made life a lot easier if you could find something you had in common with Paul, if he thought you'd had similar experiences in life as he had he would be on your wavelength.

Speaking about the call outs we would get I saw that Paul used to bully his kids, many times his kids would come to the Wood Street Police Station counter and try to get themselves brought into police custody just to get away from their Dad, I also know of one that tried to get booked into Pinderfields as an inpatient just to get away from Paul. The lad used to say that the only place his dad wouldn't go was to the police station or onto the hospital premises. Paul's sons had reputations themselves but when Paul was out looking for them they would be in hiding in fear of him. Paul's kids certainly never had the best of life at home with him I can tell you that.

I know of Paul's father Walter, the word I got back from working on the Lupset estate was Walter Sykes was a real gentleman and a very kind man. People used to always say how wrong it was what his son had put him through. There wasn't a strong bond between Paul and Walter and I know Paul used to try to intimidate his dad a lot.

I know that when Paul started going to prison at 17 years old he was that feared that the courts upgraded him from going to a young offenders to going straight into an adult prison, Wakefield HMP, which is for men.

Paul's hands were very scary looking they were as big as dinner plates and bigger than my feet!

There was an altercation on Westgate and it transpired that Paul had been fighting police officers outside of Rooftop Gardens. This was in the early 1990's. Paul was on the floor being restrained and he said he felt a punch. An officer who had seen it all said it wasn't a punch but these bobbies were fighting for their lives with him. Paul could do a colossal amount of damage with just one punch so the officer who had witnessed this allegedly kicked Paul in the head to get him to comply and to get him off these other officers.

Quite often when we had Paul Sykes in our custody or when we had him in the cells we would often substitute the arresting officer for a different officer, a different face so as Paul wasn't as volatile, we found that this approach would change Paul's attitude and he would be far more respectful to an officer who hadn't taken him there in the first place.

Us, as police, were very aware of Paul Sykes making a living as a debt collector. Paul was paid to basically to go and intimidate people and this was usually for people like Dennis Flint. Dennis used Paul many times as his enforcer and this was common knowledge across the force. Allegedly Dennis Flint had drug connections and I remember he had a big white Rolls Royce. When I first started in service we used to get paired up with another officer to learn our trade and when we would patrol Heath Common on a night in our van the old-time officer would point to Dennis' house and say, "That house over there was all built on drugs". I never had any dealings with Dennis Flint but the word from the other officers was that he was a real slippery character and always two steps ahead of the law.

The thing with Paul was that nobody necessarily wanted to put in a complaint about him. The times when we would get him was when he had been caught in the act of doing something he shouldn't have been. People would ring 999 about Paul Sykes just to get him away but they wouldn't make a statement against him. They would ring 999 on the sneak to get him locked up or moved on and most of the occasions when I got called out to Paul Sykes he was intoxicated. We used to lock him up for drunk and disorderly then and that would make the shop owners or pub owners happy. The Lupset estate had this 'no grassing' rule so this would suit everyone as there would have been serious repercussions if anyone had the balls to make a statement against Paul Sykes.

Towards the end of Paul's life his hygiene was bad and quite often Paul would urinate himself, mainly because medically he'd lost all control of his bladder. You could see his skin colour had changed too. When I first saw Paul in court he would wear a shirt and a suit, hair neatly combed with his trademark moustache but apart from that clean shaven. There wasn't a slither of that man left though at the end, everything had gone to pot for him. He had become a vulnerable adult and would sometimes need to be looked after by the police in case he caused himself any harm, sometimes the police would go out to him just to protect him from harming himself. I don't mean physically harm himself but some of the positions he put himself in through not looking after himself would put him in harm's way, he was harming himself through personal neglect. Paul wouldn't feed himself; he wouldn't go to the Doctors or hospital if he needed it. Paul was diabetic so he knew what he was doing when he drank, it was the drink that was causing him physical harm.

When Paul was ever in our custody or in hospital he would have to be washed. He couldn't be discharged in the state he was in. He was looking dishevelled and his clothes were rags. It was in his later life that he became an easy target for the youth of Wakefield, they saw him as an easy target and someone who they could use to boost their own reputations as it was common knowledge in Wakefield by this time that Paul Sykes was way past his best and he had no way of defending himself.

The drinkers and the criminals in Wakefield were another set who took full advantage of his current situation make no mistake about that. It's a crying shame really as he wasn't a well man by then not by a long shot and if it had been the Paul Sykes of old they wouldn't have gone anywhere near him, even in their gangs of 12!

In 2006 though Paul was living down Alverthorpe Road at one point and he had a fella living with him who was more or less his carer. Well, the police got a call and I had to go out on the call to find that Paul had stabbed his carer. He hadn't stabbed him the intention of killing him obviously as he'd stabbed him in the backside. This was because Paul had reacted badly to one of his jokes and we had to lock Paul up for that that night. Paul's carer dropped all charges the next day and nothing was to be done about it. I think the fella that Paul had stabbed made friends with him again and they carried on drinking together. To be honest I think Paul did that to his friend because of all the medication he was on, I think a side effect of some of his medication was that it made him that little bit extra violent if you will.

All the time Paul Sykes lived on Alverthorpe Road all the neighbours got used to the police coming down and it was because Paul was doing stupid things like stabbing his carer!

Back in the 1970's and 80's the police officers of Wakefield only had little truncheons; they didn't have CS gas so it was all hands to the pump with Paul. Every time Paul got arrested and he wanted to play up we had to send half the shift to deal with him. Paul Sykes, as far as West Yorkshire Police were concerned had a reputation of never going quietly.

You had to gain Paul's trust a little bit and then you could sit down with Paul and talk to him about anything and I'm sure they'd be many police officers in Wakefield who could back me up on this when I say that Paul's intelligence was really something else. Political news or news in the papers he knew about it and he'd give you a full and valid opinion on it and then he'd like to point out the facts and the reasons that his views were right.

Some days Paul would have his quiet days in our custody suite where he wouldn't say anything but then if the wrong person stepped in the room, like a police officer he didn't like, Paul would quickly turn angry. I found Paul to be up and down in his moods all the time and I would say he was certainly mentally unwell at points in his life. I've heard many police officers say the same.

At the end of Paul's life, he cut a very lonely figure, he knew he had lost everything that he had had and that a couple of his boys had gone to prison, many of the call outs we'd get then would be about Paul going into the bus station urinating in corners and on the children's rides.

When Paul died it was big news in the station. I think in truth Wakefield police were glad to see the back of him and I know a lot of police officers saw him as a black mark against the city.

Paul Sykes enjoyed controlling everyone around him and I think he got off on that and that can be a very dangerous trait. He controlled other people because he couldn't control himself.

Paul is still spoken about to this day in Wakefield police station. Every generation of police officer has their own rogues that they will always talk about and refer back to and Paul Sykes will not be forgotten among my generation of officers. He was a total one off and I don't think our station will see another like him again in a hurry.

Even though he only passed away ten years ago I think that he would have been dealt with differently now because society has changed. In my opinion, I think Paul should have been sectioned because he was a danger to himself and the public but I don't think he could help that, maybe if he'd had proper help with his mental illness then that danger could have been greatly reduced.

When we had to go on a job to Paul Sykes we always had to take someone with us, we had to at least in pairs and we would organise a van of officer's ready to go at a minute's notice, you'd have to get to him then make an assessment of just how many of you thought this call out was going to take and quite often there would be a gang of officers waiting around a corner waiting to see if we could get Paul to comply peacefully. If we caught him on a good day, which happened occasionally, then we could get him to come peacefully. If it was a bad day then the vans and the extra officers would be needed as Paul would cause some real damage if not contained.

I find the views in Wakefield about Paul to be split down the middle really, to some he wasted his life, wasted his talent in boxing by having it all and throwing it all away then there's some that think of Paul Sykes as a good man and a bit of a hero.

Speaking from experience on dealing with Paul over the years you wouldn't want him to be your first ever arrest if you were a new police officer. From the first time I arrested him outside Robert Ramsden's shop on Hall Road, to the last time in April 2006 for stabbing Stephen Whitely in the arse, you are talking about two completely different people. Paul ended up a polar opposite of what he had been in his youth.

I always think that Paul must have turned down so much medical help in his life, he surely must have seen a fair number of professionals in the police service and in the prison service. Paul had been before the courts many times and these courts have wide sentencing powers and they must have made it compulsory that he did some courses in moderation.

Paul just never seemed to calm down or show any improvement in his behaviour, he was always crazy.

Paul's criminal record was something else to look at, the amount of criminal convictions he had was unreal. When he started out most of his convictions were for extreme violence then at the end they would be for him wandering into shops stealing beer or food and being where his ASBO said he shouldn't be. These shops though didn't prosecute him they put their loss down to broken bottles just so they could get Paul out of their way and could carry on with their day. Who would want to spend a day in court with Paul Sykes?

I shouldn't say this but Paul used to make me laugh when I was on duty even if it was a serious matter he had that natural ability to connect with people but he just decided to be a criminal.

Paul loved the attention he would get from the media and he would often play up for them even in court if he thought it would be in the papers. You can see this if you've ever seen the last picture of Paul outside Wakefield Magistrates Court with his six coats on and scruffy beard posing for the waiting press giving it all with the 'jazz hands'. He would get a real kick from all the attention.

# THE ROAD MAN

Jack W Gregory

*Standing at the gates of the*
*prison he called home*
*The former mountain man of*
*Wakefield stands alone*
*A mere shadow of his former*
*self*
*And his life is fading and fading*
*fast*
*Not looking forward for the fear*
*of looking back*

*Eyes to the grey asphalt covered*
*ground*
*Unsteady, uneasy*
*He is Wakefield bound*

*Back to the streets*
*Back to the pain*
*Back to the place they all know*
*his name*

*Sykesy the tramp*
*Only got himself to blame*
*At least that's what they say*
*Only deserves to sleep in a*
*dilapidated doorway*
*Doesn't he?*

*His old friend Stella, she wont*
*disappoint*

*Her warm kiss will comfort him*
*Or at least keep him in a*
*slumped sedated state*
*So he could remain blissfully*
*ignorant of the forthcoming hate*

*Once a boxer of champion*
*breed*
*Who travelled the county and*
*sowed his seed*
*A life of fame stood before him*
*A bestselling book*
*Yet like so many men before*
*him*
*The drink fucked him up*

# THE LAST WORD

Chris Campbell


Now you have read the final chapters of the tales about Paul Sykes, for all you good people who have got to the end of this latest book about the 'Wild man of Wakefield' I would just like to make this statement - I am in NO WAY an expert on the life & times of Paul Sykes, I am merely a Wakefield man born & bred with a lifetime of experiences in this city and it also helps that I know most people from around here! Many folk who I know & met often crossed his path and most were happy to tell of their experiences. So, I feel that I am honoured to assist the author Jamie in his summing up of Paul's crazy life & times. So here goes...

Paul Sykes has been & gone, but he is still remembered in our city today as if it was only yesterday. Now due to the havoc & mayhem he caused he is definitely NOT remembered through 'rose tinted glasses' for the majority of people, in fact when his name is mentioned many folk still don their tin hats & run for cover! However, there are still quite a few people who never got to see the bad side of him, and as such have only good memories of him to tell.

Now in my job working as a taxi driver I get to speak to so many Wakefield people from all walks of life who still remember him for good, bad or maybe 'other' reasons. But as soon as his name cropped up in my cab it always ensured that I didn't get the usual boring three questions that drive us cab drivers' crackers - Been busy then mate? What time do you start/finish? Aaargh! But then their tales of 'Sykesy' would ensue, which always made the journey more entertaining as I listened to their stories...

But whilst he was still 'At Large' it didn't matter which part of the city it was, it could have been Lupset, Eastmoor, Peacock, Portobello or anywhere - but when I picked my passengers up if Sykesy had been in the vicinity, folk always had a tale to tell. Either he might have been drunk and been trying to tap money for beer or fags, or perhaps he'd nicked cans of Special Brew out of the local shop, or maybe he'd been carrying on and threatened passers-by or had been 'duffed up' by the local youths again, but no matter what, there was ALWAYS a story about him to hear!

As a percentage of people who I have spoken to, either folk who I know or who I pick up in my taxi regarding Paul, I would say that about 25% have positive memories of him and miss his passing - but I'd say that a VERY large 75% were glad to see the back of him, and a lot of people breathed a big sigh of relief when they knew that he'd finally gone! Alas he still leaves a legacy behind though as there are still a lot of folk who are unwilling to talk about him. Some are still afraid of the stigma that was attached to him, and the threat that any of his surviving family or cohorts might maybe appear & do them a bad turn maybe, and indeed, the mere mention of his name still gives some people the shivers, as if he might pop up from the 'Afterlife' and haunt them!

However, there are many more people who I know that do NOT have those fears, but due to their professions they felt that they could not contribute due to being restricted by the 'data protection & patient confidentiality' acts. I have heard many stories from these currently still serving Police & Prison officers and Ambulance personnel, who I know personally regarding Mr Sykes. But sadly, I cannot reiterate their experiences as they felt that they could not contribute to the book due to the aforementioned laws which is a great pity, as I heard some very interesting stories & scenarios!

I can quote things told to me by a few Wakefield characters who are proper 'old school' geezers who I have spoken to but who sadly will have to remain nameless. I was hoping to get them to chat to Jamie and add a chapter for this book, but whilst telling me many fascinating tales about Paul for reasons of their own they didn't want to write a chapter or to get involved. A couple didn't want to tell tales 'Out of school' or 'Speak ill of the dead' as they said, and one in particular said that Paul Sykes' brought back too many bad memories which were better off left dead & buried. He is afraid that if he told his tales that the ghost of Sykesy might again be resurrected & folk would then seek him out to hear his stories, which he does NOT want as he prefers to forget the past, as he says he prefers the quiet life & keeps a low profile these days!

Now some of these geezers told me some very fascinating tales. All these men did time with Paul and their stories included shotguns, a crossbow, and a particular legendary story from Wakefield folklore regarding the misappropriate use of a bar stool, resulting in Sykesy ending up in the intensive care unit! But as the story also goes, Sykesy didn't care for hospital food so he signed himself out as soon as he woke up properly the next day. Also, another story was whilst one of these men was in Liverpool jail doing time alongside Sykesy, he witnessed a violent punch up between Sykesy and another con on one of the wing landings, which involved the other geezer bodily picking Paul up & throwing him over the landing railings where he then ended up bouncing about like he was on a trampoline on the suicide safety meshing!

However, I must say that in my honest opinion that there will never be another character of the likes of Paul Sykes, well certainly not in Wakefield ever again. The man left a legacy of fear & dread amongst many people, some who can sadly NEVER tell of their stories due to shame or pure humiliation. However, as I have previously mentioned, a few people never met the 'Psycho Paul' they only ever met the 'Positive Paul' and as such only have happy memories of him.

Which brings me now to his 'Final Curtain' - The last time I ever saw Paul Sykes alive was maybe only a couple of weeks before he passed away. Now at the time I was working for a taxi firm called Diamond Cars who at the time had the NHS & hospital contracts. I had got the call from control to go & pick up an old lady who had had a fall from Pinderfields hospital A&E, and could I please go in & give her assistance as they were short staffed and she needed help walking.

So, I got to the A&E and went in & found my passenger. Now she could not walk properly so I went & got a wheelchair for her and got her sat in it. Now as I was wheeling her through the waiting room everyone turned around as an ambulance had just arrived. So then through the doors walked two members of the ambulance crew holding up a tall but very broken looking bearded skeleton. Now it was obvious then that this was Paul, but he was in such a bad state that you would never believe that the skeleton had once been him. His face was battered and his eyes were blackened & swollen to such a state that I dare say that he would not have been able to see out of them, and his hair & beard were totally unkempt and he smelled REALLY bad! He stunk like the sewers and it was obvious that he'd been using the toilet, but he had obviously forgotten to remove his trousers first!

He was covered in eggshells as he'd obviously been used for target practice again, and due to the state of him it looked like the brave youths of our city had decided to give him another kicking as he seemed to be either punch drunk, blind drunk or a mixture of both. But whatever it was he was still partly conscious as he was sort of growling and shouting the words 'Bastards, bastards, the fucking bastards' So he had probably been used as a football again and been kicked around the park. But whether he was concussed or paralytic at the time, the taking of Paul Sykes' scalp when he was at this stage in his life was NOTHING for any young 'wannabes' to boast about, so I sincerely hope they have not!

But as many many people have said that in later life Paul Sykes got exactly what he deserved. Karma turned through 360 degrees and he got his - he got his 'just desserts' - However I just wonder how many young lads who are reading this now might have been one of the many who gave him some boot or used him for target practice, and if they ever regret doing what they did? As in my opinion even though the bully ended up getting bullied himself, however two wrongs never make a right. So, if YOU are one of those lads who gave him a beating do you regret it, or do you somehow feel it was 'justified violence?'

So, to end my contribution I would say that I can only compare the shell of the man that remained to the prime physical example that I once had those confrontations with all those many years before. But all I can really think of in this situation is 'how the once mighty have fallen' - and how Karma comes back round to punish people for what they have done in their past maybe?

So, from 1946 to 2007 the world was home to a definite 'character' now either you loved him or hated him, but one thing is for sure - there will NEVER be another like Paul Sykes. The good lord certainly threw the mould away after he was created. So, rest in peace Paul Sykes... for reasons good or bad, you will certainly NEVER be forgotten!

# A LIFE OF AGONY

Chris Campbell

*There is a nickname for us Yorkshiremen, we are known as 'Tykes'*
*But the toughest and most feared, was a man name of Paul Sykes*
*He was a Wakefield man from an estate, that is named 'Lupset'*
*And sadly there are many folk on there, who he managed to upset*

*Born in the year of 1946, the son of Walter and Betty,*
*As a lad he turned to crime, the first of which were petty*
*Whilst young he was bashed and belted, the son of a wicked Dad,*
*But getting beaten every day, is that why he turned out bad?*

*As a need to 'act the hard man' Paul Sykes could shed no tears,*
*Maybe that's why he went off the rails, whilst in his younger years?*
*He rebelled against the system, and acted more uncouth,*
*So is that why he turned to violence, whist still in his youth?*

*Assaulting folk and robbing, and more serious crime,*
*It wasn't long as a young man, that Paul was 'doing time'*
*Making threats to kill and violence, so early in his life,*
*He created trouble daily, and caused people so much strife*

*But his violent tendencies were seen as a potential for boxing,*
*He soon found his vocation, where he had much talent 'in the ring'*
*During his amateur career, his opponents he mostly pasted,*
*Alas in his later life, all his skills and talents Paul he wasted*

*Then he turned 'Pro' and signed up with manager Tommy Miller,*
*The pundits said he could go 'all the way, Sykesy he's a killer!'*
*As a heavyweight contender, Sykes became a famous name,*
*And knocking out opponents, that soon became his game*

As a pro boxer, Paul Sykes was a 'Big Hitter' in the ring,
Who could have foreseen the future, or the mayhem he would bring?
But his boxing career by the 'Old Bill' sometimes it was curtailed,
Which often meant that Sykesy, he ended up back getting jailed

Whilst he was drunk, Sykesy terrorised the neighbourhood
But when sobered up, he claimed he was just 'misunderstood!'
Now Sykesy was a Wakefield man, Lupset born and bred,
but in his violent heyday, he was mostly 'off his head!'

In Heppy's or Dolly Gray's nightclubs, drunk or high as a kite,
He'd just pick on any bloke, any excuse to cause a fight
Once on a lifelong friend he took on a £200-pound contract,
Then attacked him in Heppy's, what a dirty low-down act!

Arrested again for violence, with no chance of getting bail,
'Take him down' said Judge Pickles 'straight back to Armley jail!'
For anyone in authority or uniform, Paul Sykes he was bad news,
He served 21 years in prison, for attacking coppers and the screws!

On the inside Sykesy was the 'Daddy' of that there was no doubt,
However, there were lots of dodgy rumours, about the 'Lupset Lout!'
Stories that he liked 'Man Fun' - many rumours they abounded,
But were these allegations true, or were they totally unfounded?

Paul was Institutionalised but happy, whilst he was inside,
And wrote his book 'Sweet Agony' with a jailbird's sense of pride
Regarding intellect, a more clever man you wouldn't likely meet,
But on the outside, you wouldn't like to meet him on the street!

When he was released from jail, he sparred Joe Frazier in the ring,
And also Leon Spinks, financed by the promoter named 'Don King'
Due to prison and his fitness, Paul was in prime physical condition
And so, after a few fights, he was ranked in a 'Contender' position

Sykesy was a fighter, and from what was the first bell,
He came out throwing punches, and he gave opponents hell!
As a boxer he was talented, but was known to be a cheat,

'Cos he'd resort to 'fighting dirty' to avoid him getting beat

If he was under pressure, and his opponent showed no fear,
He'd do a 'Tyson special' like when Mike bit Holyfield's ear!
In March '78 for the British central area heavyweight title fight,
He was disqualified against Neil Malpass, for 'dirty fighting' that night

'Box clever Paul' his seconds shouted 'Malpass on points he is ahead'
Back in the corner they told him to 'use his boxing head'
But behind and under pressure, Sykesy showed he had 'No Class'
He went straight out next round, and 'Stuck the Nut' on Neil Malpass!

Now Sykesy he had boxing talent, of that there was no doubt,
But scaring folk and violence, that's what he was all about
Whilst as a boxer he could fight, and he certainly could slug,
But in real life he just bullied people, he was nothing but a thug

Whilst fighting John. L. Gardener, Paul Sykes ran out of gas,
He surrendered like Roberto Duran, when he said, 'No Mas'
John. L. was overwhelming him, in an 'all out' attack,
So in round 6 Sykesy just gave up, the coward turned his back!

Paul Sykes, he once had talent, and he could have been a 'Champ'
but he ended up a down and out, nothing but a tramp
His talents they were wasted, and everyone they knew,
That rather than go training, he'd drink 10 cans of Special Brew!

From Wakefield city centre, Paul got many 'ASBO' bans,
From drinking too much cider, and that special brew in cans
He slept rough in the bus station, abusing people with his rants,
And ended up incontinent, messing up his pants

For beer or fags the 'passersby' he would constantly harass,
And whilst 'blind drunk' the local yokels liked to knock him on his ass
He'd stand there and swear and shout, unsteady on his legs,
Whilst they used him for target practice, and pelted him with eggs!

*His hair was set on fire whilst sleeping on a park bench, in a cowardly attack,*
*And lots of people said it was Karma, paying him right back!*
*But Paul was asleep when they burned him, and no-one was ever blamed,*
*Those cowards with the lighter fuel, they should be 'Named and Shamed!'*

*He ended just a bearded vagrant, with a massive pair of hands,*
*Drunk and threatening passersby, who no-one understands*
*In the precinct he was a menace, he used to curse and shout,*
*But he died a broken shell of a man, of that there is no doubt*

*So, from a heavyweight contender, who was 'In Drink' a nutter,*
*Paul Sykes ended up a tramp, just a vagrant in the gutter*
*Many young lads boasted of the famous scalp, that they had just claimed,*
*but it always took a few of them, to leave poor Sykesy hurt and maimed*

*Always drunk and disorderly, Paul would stagger about and lurch,*
*But he was guided somehow, to find peace at Wakefield Methodist Church*
*He was seeking solace for each jail sentence, and for every prison cell,*
*As no doubt he knew he was fast approaching, his own 'final bell'*

*But since he has passed over, he now has the ultimate ASBO,*
*He's now in the 'spirit world' where no-one wants to go*
*The church they tried their hardest, but Paul they couldn't save,*
*He now resides in St Paul's churchyard Alverthorpe, buried in an early grave*

*R.I.P. Paul Sykes*
*1946 - 2007*

# AFTERWORD

Jamie Boyle

Paul Sykes' book 'Sweet Agony' was written in 1988 and it won the Arthur Koestler Award in the same year, eventually being published in 1990. Sweet Agony is about Paul's life from 1976 to 1979 and following its re-release in 2015 there has been a resurgence of interest in Paul Sykes.

After setting up my 'Paul Sykes' social media pages I saw for myself just how much people wanted to know about him. There was a mixture of interest, there were the youngsters who had seen the clips of him on YouTube talking about punching sharks to the older generation who sometimes had heated discussions on my page and boxing forums as to whether or not Paul would have beat Lenny McLean back in November 1979 when they were supposed to fight in an unlicensed boxing fight.

Following on from my own interest in Paul Sykes, which came about in the summer of 2012, I decided to do some research as to what had happened to this huge character. I couldn't find out anything really and I was surprised that no one had written a book about him already, that is what led me to write 'Sykes – Unfinished Agony' which I'm pleased to say went on to be an Amazon Best Seller and received some fabulous reviews as well as the odd death threat but then you can't please everyone!

Sykes – Further Agony has come about because, such was the interest in Paul now, that I was getting messaged by people wanting to tell me their stories about him, I couldn't just ignore some of the things that were told to me and that was when I decided there had to be a second book.

Paul Sykes was someone who courted attention and it seems it's still the same today, he still has a magnetic effect, people are drawn to hearing about him, talking about him and reading about him.

Of course, these books have had a mixed reception as Paul did himself in life but I am delighted to let you all know that these books have been picked up by Western Edge Pictures who are going to be making a new documentary and a film about Paul's life story. Vaughan Sivell from Western Edge Pictures, who is an award-winning Producer, Director and Writer has been as enthralled as everyone who has read these books. Vaughan said that he knew the moment that he'd watched the Paul Sykes at Large documentary and realised that no one else had done anything on Paul Sykes that he was going to bring him to the big screen.

Vaughan won three BAFTA's Cymru Awards which included the award for Best Director (factual)for his movie 'Mr Calzaghe' which is a film about the unbeaten Welsh boxer Joe Calzaghe. He has recently finished filming 'Pistorius' the story of the Paralympic and Olympic athlete and convicted murderer which is set against the political backdrop of South Africa. The film is represented by Content Media and is set for release late in 2017.

I can't tell you how excited I am that all three books are going to be merged to piece together his life in what is sure to be a fantastic film, so keep a look out folks, next stop Leicester Square!

Finally, I'll explain why this book wasn't called 'Sykes – Final Agony'. Final Agony would have meant that the door was closed for me to write anything else about this colourful character. Who knows what the future holds, but for me this is the last book that I plan to write about Paul but you just don't know who will come forward next with another story that just has to be told. I imagine that if there was to be another one it would have to come from his immediate family, and that is something that I wouldn't hold my breath on but like I said you never know.

Thanks for the support you have all shown me, it's been immense, I've had messages from all over the world from people who have been following my journey, it's all been quite overwhelming. Many thanks, always a pleasure.

## ALSO AVAILABLE FROM WARCRY PRESS

**Sweet Agony by Paul Sykes**
*ISBN - 978 0995531222*

The original book penned by Paul himself whilst in Hull
Prison, outlining his life in and out of Prison and eventual
rise to the John L Gardner fight.

**Unfinished Agony by Jamie Boyle**
*ISBN - 978 0995531246*

*The first instalment of the Paul Sykes interviews,
and Amazon Best Seller*

**WARCRY PRESS**